Perfectly Human

Perfectly Human

Nine Months with Cerian

Sarah C. Williams

Plough Publishing House

Published by Plough Publishing House
Walden, New York
Robertsbridge, England
Elsmore, Australia
www.plough.com

Plough produces books, a quarterly magazine, and Plough.com to encourage
people and help them put their faith into action. We believe Jesus can transform
the world and that his teachings and example apply to all aspects of life. At the
same time, we seek common ground with all people regardless of their creed.

Plough is the publishing house of the Bruderhof, an international community
of families and singles seeking to follow Jesus together. Members of the Bruderhof
are committed to a way of radical discipleship in the spirit of the Sermon on the
Mount. Inspired by the first church in Jerusalem (Acts 2 and 4), they renounce
private property and share everything in common in a life of nonviolence, justice,
and service to neighbors near and far. To learn more about the Bruderhof's faith,
history, and daily life, see Bruderhof.com. (Views expressed by Plough authors are
their own and do not necessarily reflect the position of the Bruderhof.)

ISBN: 978-0-87486-669-8
22 21 20 19 18   2 3 4 5 6 7 8

Cover image copyright © 2018 by Kyle Hartsock
Original title: *The Shaming of the Strong: The Challenge of an Unborn Life*
Scripture quotations are from THE HOLY BIBLE, NEW INTERNATIONAL
VERSION®, NIV® Copyright © 1973, 1978, 1984, 2011 by Biblica, Inc.® Used by
permission. All rights reserved worldwide.

A catalog record for this book is available from the British Library.
Library of Congress Cataloging-in-Publication Data
Names: Williams, Sarah C. (Sarah Charlotte), 1968- author.
Title: Perfectly human : nine months with Cerian / Sarah C. Williams.
Other titles: Shaming of the strong
Description: Walden, New York : Plough Publishing House, [2017]
Identifiers: LCCN 2018006764 (print) | LCCN 2018021954 (ebook) | ISBN
    9780874866926 (epub) | ISBN 9780874867305 (mobi) | ISBN 9780874867466 (
    pdf) | ISBN 9780874866698 (paperback)
Subjects: LCSH: Stillbirth--Religious aspects--Christianity. |
    Abortion--Religious aspects--Christianity. | Pregnancy--Psychological
    aspects. | Bereavement--Psychological aspects.
Classification: LCC BV4907 (ebook) | LCC BV4907 .W58 2017 (print) | DDC
    248.8/66092 [B] --dc23
LC record available at https://lccn.loc.gov/2018006764

Printed in the United States of America

Contents

I

The Day of Trouble

There are two entrances to the Women's Center at the John
Radcliffe Hospital in Oxford. We took the top one. I glanced
at my watch as we entered the lobby. My calculations had
been precise. I had ten minutes to spare before my routine
twenty-week ultrasound scan in the Prenatal Diagnosis Unit.
I had dropped the children at school, driven to the supermarket to do the week's shopping, rushed home, crammed
the food into the cupboards and begun preparations for
Hannah's birthday party later that afternoon. All day I had
been reminiscing about the birth of our eldest exactly eight
years before. Hannah was born in Canada on Vancouver's
North Shore in a room that overlooked the white-capped
mountains of Grouse and Seymour. I remembered the
mountains as I struggled to purchase my parking ticket.

My neighbor was on the seventh floor of the John
Radcliffe, having given birth to her third baby thirty-six
hours earlier. I headed straight for the lift, abandoning my
mother in the lobby. I found Adrienne sitting up in bed like
a queen, radiant with the relief and joy of her son's arrival. I
held him in my arms and realized with a surge of excitement
that this would soon be me. I laughed out loud as I headed

back to the ground floor. Next time I visited the seventh floor I would have my baby with me.

The waiting room was surprisingly full for a Monday afternoon. My mother set up her laptop to catch up on some work. Paul would have done the same if he had been here, instead of in a client meeting in London. He and I had never been sentimental about ultrasounds. The first time we had seen Hannah on the screen in the Lion's Gate Hospital in Vancouver, we both reacted to the bizarre unreality of seeing our child for the first time through the intrusive medium of technology. Our friends had told us this would be the moment of bonding, but we struggled to tell the difference between a head and a foot, our eyes flitting back and forth between graphs and cursors. The image on the screen bore little relation to the clear mental picture we had of our child. We vowed never to have another ultrasound scan and we discussed the ethics of prenatal screening all the way home in our clapped-out Dodge Omni. Such conversations came naturally to us during our student days.

Perhaps I was mellowing with age or maybe the exhaustion of two small children had taken the edge off my idealism; either way I could barely read the magazine in front of me I was so excited to see our baby by whatever means.

The doctor called my name and I got up to follow him. He asked my mother to join us. Not wishing to overstep any grandmotherly boundaries, she was reluctant at first, but sharing my enthusiasm she did not take much persuasion.

It was dark in the room and I remember the dull pattern on the curtain around the bed and the sharp cold of the jelly as the doctor squeezed it onto my bump. I made a joke about twins.

And then I saw the foot. There were no shifting lines this time; even the toes were distinct. The baby seemed for an instant to look straight at me. I could see the detail of the face. I caught my breath, silenced by a sudden rush of love and connection. I now knew what those friends meant by bonding. With Hannah it happened when I saw the bright blue line on the home pregnancy test, and with Emilia when I first held her in my arms after an arduous labor. I smiled at myself, unashamedly sentimental lying there oozing love at the screen.

"It makes it all worthwhile, doesn't it?" my mother said, reflecting my own thoughts and referring to the acute nausea that had dominated the pregnancy up until this point.

But the doctor's cheery voice gave way to a clipped monotone. He left the room and returned with a female technician. I assumed he was simply inexperienced at doing ultrasounds, and I shuffled into a sitting position and looked at my watch. I'd seen everything I wanted to see and it was time to get home to prepare the party. I bristled with irritation as the woman redid everything the doctor had done. If we didn't leave soon, there would be no time for Paul to play an extended game with the girls as planned, and to read an extra chapter of Narnia before bed.

The woman put her hand on my arm and said the words that every expectant mother hopes she will never hear: "I am so sorry. There is something wrong with the baby. We need to fetch the consultant."

"But there can't be," I responded immediately. "I saw the face. The baby looks fine to me."

She shook her head and squeezed my arm.

I went cold all over. The rational part of my brain observed this creeping paralysis from a distance with a

strange forensic clarity. How could this be? God knew I
could not bear this, not after all I'd been through.

"Mum, I'm terrified." I whispered.

"I'm going to pray." The edge in my mother's voice
suggested she was no less afraid than I was, but the discipline of years had made prayer reflexive.

I was so glad she was there. She hadn't planned to come
to the hospital with me. I'd told her I was quite content
to have some time alone, but she'd run after me as I shut
the front door. "Hang my emails! Let's make a jaunt of it.
I'll drive so you can relax and get your energies up for the
birthday party."

I heard footsteps in the corridor and the lowered tones of
serious discussion. Somehow I had to pull my mind into gear
to ask all the right questions – the questions Paul would have
asked had he been there.

The consultant sat down beside me. He checked the
notes before he spoke – evidently, my name had not featured
in the relay of information behind the door. A number of
people stood behind him peering over his shoulder at the
screen. Using the cursor and his finger for reinforcement, he
highlighted different points of the tiny person inside me and
murmured incomprehensible numbers at the group.

"I have to tell you, Mrs. Williams, this baby will not live.
It has thanatophoric dysplasia, a lethal skeletal deformity
that will certainly result in death shortly after birth. The
chest is too small to sustain the proper development of the
lungs. When the baby is born it will not be able to breathe."

I concentrated on the medical terms, repeating *thanatophoric dysplasia* over and over again under my breath. I
wanted him to stop speaking but I was too afraid of forget-
ting the words. I shouted at him in my head: "This can't be

true. You must be mistaken. You've muddled my body up with someone else. This is not my baby. It must be a fault on the screen."

But the consultant left no room for misunderstanding, the implications were plain, and I found myself nodding like everyone else in the room, intimidated by the finality of his words. "I suggest you come back with your partner in the morning and we will talk further about what you want to do."

It was not until I sat in a side room with a second consultant that I understood what was meant by "what you want to do." I listened while the doctor suggested dates for a termination.

Dazed, we made our way back through the waiting room. It is strange the detail one remembers in moments of crisis; the blond child on the floor playing with a tractor, the girl in the bright red maternity dress drinking from the water fountain, the look of pity on the receptionist's face as she watched us leave. At the exit we passed a woman leaning on her heavily swollen stomach between long drags on her cigarette. I could not speak.

My mother took my arm and steered me to the car. I crumpled into the passenger seat, remembering the delight on Paul's face when I had told him I was pregnant for the third time. We'd waited so long for this. I thought of the party balloons already taped to the letterbox and I thought of Adrienne with her arms full of her son. An aching emptiness enveloped me. Every line of thought ended with the same conclusion: "Thanatophoric dysplasia; this child will not live, it will not live . . ." Around and around it went in my head like a mantra.

Shivering uncontrollably, I wrapped my arms around my body and wished that I could disappear. I was going home to face the hardest decision of my life.

2

Pineapples and Amethysts

If praying somehow constitutes a beginning, then Christmas Day was certainly the start of it. It was then that Paul and I asked God to give us the gift of another child. December 25 has particular romantic connotations for us. Paul's uncle was the pastor of a small village church in Kent. The family had come up from Dorset to celebrate together. My family had been attending the church for some years and I had heard a great deal about "the nephew" who was studying politics, philosophy, and economics at Oxford. I did not realize at the time, however, that he had also heard a great deal about the serious girl with long blonde hair and masses of brothers and sisters who was on her way to study history at Oxford.

Paul sat four pews in front of my sprawling family. We were so many that we took up two rows, forming a human bloc on one side the church. Half of us were presided over by my mother, and the other half were supervised by my harassed father. I sat sandwiched between Naomi and Justyn on this particular morning, with my youngest brother Richard squirming on my lap. At the end of the second hymn Paul turned around and our eyes met for a second only. I hid behind Richard for the rest of the service, overcome by shyness.

Exactly seventeen years later we stood in the pouring rain halfway up a Welsh hillside searching for an ancient Celtic pilgrim site. For some reason it mattered to us to pray for another child at this particular site. My historical zeal matched Paul's keen sense of Welsh ancestry and we pressed on up the hill regardless of the rain.

The fact that Christians had been praying on this hill for the best part of two millennia was lost on the rest of the family, wet, cold, and hungry for Christmas turkey. "Can't you pray by the wood burner?" they pleaded.

"Of course we can," I said, "but it wouldn't be . . ." I struggled to find the right word, "as poetic." Paul and I had been waiting five long years and we were not going to be thwarted.

After Emilia was born, the doctor told us that we would be extremely unwise to contemplate having any more children. A long-term back injury had become acute as a result of the pregnancy. I had spent three months in bed after Emilia was born but it was a year before I could lift her into her cot at night. If my disc were to prolapse again I was likely to face major back surgery. We waited, and meanwhile I watched my friends have their thirds and fourths, lifting them effortlessly from car seat to stroller or into swings at the playground, wielding vacuum cleaners, and stooping at the end of the day to pick up toys without even bending their knees. Some of them began to ask if Paul and I had given up on having more children. Slowly, I revised my expectations and reassessed the enduring assumption Paul and I had harbored since we were first married, of having at least four children.

It felt like a declaration of defeat when I finally admitted I needed sustained help to cope with the two I already had. It was at this stage that Emma came to nanny for us. We had known Emma since she was eighteen. She and her family had been part of our church in Oxford and we had observed her gentle consistency over the years as she had served as a nanny for one family after another. I could hardly believe our good fortune when she agreed to come and work for us. With inimitable efficiency she took on a large part of the physical work of caring for the children while I immersed myself in work. Spending three years teaching at Birmingham University before returning to Oxford to take up a History Fellowship at one of the University Colleges, I persisted with my back exercises and we continued to hope.

And, after five years, we reached Christmas Day and the wet pilgrim site. I know that God can hear prayer anywhere, but there was something special about that hillside and perhaps God saw the funny, earnest side of our kneeling there in the mud, holding the ancient cross, carved in the rock over a thousand years ago.

A month later, when we'd fully recovered from the colds we contracted in Wales, I was able to tell Paul he was going to be a father again. Hannah and Emilia were delirious with excitement and so was Emma.

It was with a touch of triumph that I told my closest friend our news.

"Janet, I'm pregnant," I said it abruptly in the hope I might surprise her.

"I thought you might be," she replied, as astute as ever. Her slow smile and the twinkle of humor in her eyes betrayed a coincidence of timing which reduced us both to helpless laughter. "So am I," she whispered.

We'd had our first children together. We'd read all the same books to prepare, we wanted the same things for them, and we worried about them with similar levels of intensity. Janet's eldest, Josie, and Hannah were in the same class at school, as were Emilia and Janet's third daughter, Becky. Our husbands relished the long established tradition of enjoying a celebratory drink together after the birth of each of our daughters. When Hannah was born Mark and Janet flew all the way to Canada with three-month-old Josie. Any other friends requesting a three-week stay in our small student apartment just after the birth of a baby would have met with a flat no; but not these friends. We had known them since our undergraduate days at Oxford. They were more than family to us.

Janet and I spent the rest of the day making plans, discussing due dates, and anticipating the exploits of the next two. The children retreated to the sandpit at the bottom of the yard, and Paul and Mark found urgent business to attend to elsewhere.

But then I started to be sick. I vomited first during a tutorial on Gladstone's foreign policy. I just caught a glimpse of the student's bewildered face as I fled from the classroom at high speed. I sprinted down the corridor past the senior common room where, to my horror, the principal, the senior tutor, and the college secretary were assembled for a meeting with the door open. They looked up disapprovingly, probably expecting to see an unruly undergraduate. I tried to slow my pace to a composed walk but with one hand pressed over my mouth I was anything but convincing.

Little did I realize then how many more embarrassing moments were to follow. When I returned to my study, I told the student it was something I'd eaten – it was true in a manner of speaking.

"Shall we carry on?" I mumbled, still tasting the vomit in my mouth with the distinctive metallic aftertaste of pregnancy.

"Where were we . . . ? Yes . . . To what extent can Gladstonian Liberalism be defined in terms of a distinctive foreign policy?"

"Are you all right, Dr. Williams? Do you want me to come back later?"

"Not at all! I'm absolutely fine." I said it rather too brightly. I tried my best to navigate my way around the late nineteenth century while the room heaved and the bookshelves swam in front of my eyes.

When the same thing happened twice the following week, the student began to eye me with suspicion. By the eighth week of pregnancy work was impossible. I barely moved except from my bed to the toilet to empty my sick bowl.

"Be thankful," people kept saying. "Nausea is a sign of a healthy baby." So I tried hard to be grateful imagining the baby literally brimming with good health while I wasted away. When I started to vomit on my own saliva there was nothing else to do except lie in hospital being intravenously rehydrated. It would not have been so bad if I could have read, but the words would not keep still on the page. I reeled like a novice sailor on the high seas.

When I look back I'm surprised to find that this period of intense and incapacitating sickness lasted only three months. It felt like a lifetime. Perhaps if I had known then that this is exactly what it was, I might have treasured those days more.

All this time to pray, I wrote in my journal, *but I don't know what to say.* I asked God to stop the sickness nearly as many times as I was sick. Visitors were quick to offer theories but hyperemesis is impossible to understand unless you've been through it. Sissel, my Norwegian friend, was one of the few people who really understood. Even after twenty years she had not forgotten the horror of it. "You feel so absolutely ill, like the worst sick bug you can ever remember lasting for months on end, but technically you're not ill so everyone thinks you're complaining. It is so frustrating."

"And it's not fair!" I stormed at her. "I thought we were meant to bloom in pregnancy!"

She laughed: "Another myth people put on women, I'm afraid."

I resented the fact that the small statistical minority upon whom that myth was founded seemed to cross my path with unnatural frequency, and I ranted at the injustice of men who – from my perspective – enjoyed the best moments of the procreative process but successfully avoided the painful consequences. Paul's eyes would crinkle into an ironic smile after such rants as he quietly washed out my sick bowl and prepared for yet another scintillating evening listening to my lament.

Dependency was not a word I welcomed in my vocabulary. It was the sense of helplessness that made those early days so disorientating. I ordered my life. The only way to juggle my various commitments at home and work was to fine-tune the organization of my diary, and endless vomiting did not fit with my plan. The seeming failure of both prayer and pills frustrated me beyond the resources of my humor and I found myself lower than I had been in many years and yet guilty for feeling ambivalent about something I wanted so much. I hated hearing how others were teaching my students at college, watching other people cook meals and clean our house, and looking on while the girls ran to Emma when things went wrong. All I could do was reflect, and this made me bleak.

I thought a lot about my own childhood, wondering how on earth my mother managed to have six children in ten years seemingly without batting an eyelid. I remembered the riotous fun of family walks, of debating around the kitchen table or acting a play that one of us had written. My mother had reveled in it, and to me a big family represented the pinnacle of true femininity. I guess I assumed that I would be a capable mother in the mold of my own mother. Yet the truth was, all the pregnancies had been hard and my back injury had made the early stages of child rearing a test of physical endurance, not a pleasure. This confusion of mind simply reinforced my bewilderment.

Pineapple will forever remind me of this confused feeling of dependence. Liz, our pastor's wife, phoned to ask if there was anything we needed.

"No," I said. "We're fine, thanks."

She was wise enough to add, "Are you sure?"

"Well," I murmured after a few moments, "I really fancy some pineapple."

I expected Liz to stop by with a pineapple in a couple of days; I was taken aback when, an hour later, our pastor Mike arrived on the doorstep with a glass bowl of finely cut pineapple. I had always found myself tongue-tied in Mike's presence, so there was nothing new when I stammered my thanks. His pastoral professionalism intimidated me at the best of times, and I was standing there in my old dressing-gown feeling like death.

"Go and lie back down on the sofa," Mike instructed.

I did as I was told. Taking the pineapple from him, I ate three pieces and promptly threw up in the green dishpan I kept constantly by my side. I hardly dared look up. But Mike did not flinch. Without a single platitude he picked up the sick bowl, took it to the bathroom, emptied it, cleaned it out, and laid it back down beside me on the sofa. He then went and diverted the children from their rioting with a game.

I was so stunned at the simplicity and tenderness of his actions that I stayed on the sofa. When Paul got home and took charge of the children, Mike prayed with me. There was a gentleness, which I had never seen in him before. My stereotype of "busy-self-important-pastor-with-big-black-diary-crammed-full-of-pressing-meetings" evaporated there and then. My dependency drew care from others.

My one comfort in the morass was anticipating the person I was struggling to bring into the world. I got through vomit after vomit by saying over and over again, "It will all be worth it in the end." I used to go to sleep at night imagining our child and thinking how I would look back and laugh at all the sickness when I held the baby in my arms. Janet came often during those weeks, taking the girls off to play or just sitting with me, cheering me up with the anticipation of shared joy.

"Hello, darling, it's Wren," came the voice at the other end of the telephone. My mother called herself Wren with all the family these days. Paul had first adopted the nickname years ago as a way of avoiding the difficult dilemma of how to address his new mother-in-law. Should he call her "Mum" like her own children, "Jen" like the rest of her family, "Jenny" like her friends, or "Jennifer" like the bank manager. He opted for "Wren" as in the children's story *Jenny Wren;* and thereafter the name stuck. "I've been praying for the baby," she said "and I had a vivid picture. Can I tell you about it?"

"Of course, go ahead." I needed all the encouragement I could get.

"There's a little mountain stream behind the family home in Scotland where I used to play as a child. Hard granite boulders containing layers of amethyst come tumbling down into the water and the amethyst layers are exposed. These layers are very soft and fragile and they don't look like amethyst; in fact it's hard to tell them apart from any other stone. But if you put them in a pebble polisher they come out looking like jewels. Maybe this baby is like an amethyst. Perhaps the beauty is not easy to see at first but inside there will be something unexpected and intensely beautiful but also fragile. The beauty may need to be carefully honed before it is apparent to others."

When our conversation ended I searched for the amethyst necklace my father gave me when I was nine. He'd taken the stone from this same stream in Scotland. I kept it by my bed to remind me of the treasure and to help me appreciate the beauty in spite of the vomit.

By week twenty I had some of my energy back and apart from the unrelenting feeling of sickness I was much recovered, if a little thinner than normal. I even ventured into the attic to take a sneak preview of the baby clothes. Somewhere inside me I harbored the belief that I had earned an easy second half to the pregnancy. I began to anticipate cashing in on a late bloom. I was even cheery when Paul lay in bed with pneumonia, glad that I could do something for him at last. I remember, with a shudder of irony, writing in my journal: *The worst is over. Now I can start looking forward.*

3

A Question

I sat bolt upright in bed, my hair soaked with sweat. I clutched my tummy out of instinct. It was still dark outside although I could just hear a few birds starting to sing. Paul was fast asleep next to me. I crept out of our room and fumbled through the darkness, making my way downstairs to the kitchen where I made myself a cup of tea.

At first I couldn't remember my dream, only the atmosphere of it. It was the overarching sense of foreboding that had woken me. The house was coming down on my head, or to be more precise it was bending under the strain of a terrific hurricane. In my dream I'd been standing under the archway between the kitchen and the back door where I now stood waiting for the kettle to boil. The entire building swayed and bowed, forcing me to the ground where I lay praying the storm would pass but expecting the roof to collapse on me.

And that was it. I'd woken up, sure it was real.

I hugged my cup of tea and rubbed my tummy. I had always dreamed vividly during pregnancy.

Emilia had heard my descent and she trundled into the kitchen with Teddy under her arm. She snuggled on my lap, sipped the cooling dregs of my tea, and took a surprisingly long time to remember it was Hannah's birthday. She burst into the inevitable flurry of excited activity as soon as she remembered, and together we attached balloons to the light over the table, laid the table with birthday napkins, and arranged cards and small presents around Hannah's place, putting the larger ones carefully to one side to be opened that evening.

By six o'clock we were ready for Paul and Hannah to wake up and join our fun. We had to resort to the smell of chocolate to rouse them both and even then it was some time before we all sat up in our bed, Emilia and I with considerably more enthusiasm than the other two.

"How are we going to fit five in this bed?" Paul groaned.

Emilia pressed her mouth to my tummy and shouted, "Say 'Happy Birthday' to your sister, baby!"

Hannah put her head on my shoulder and asked me quietly what time she was born. "When am I actually eight?"

"Not until 7:23 tonight," I said.

"But that was Canada time," Paul interjected. "If you really want to be accurate about it, Han, you were born early on the morning of the fourteenth of May, English time, so it is not your birthday today after all."

"I am Canadian, I suppose."

Paul grinned and winked at her from the other side of the bed.

As I took the girls to school that morning I could never have anticipated how much could change in just twelve hours. I think now as I write of my friend who waved goodbye to her husband after breakfast and by afternoon was a single parent with four children under ten. I think of Tanya, who packed her son's lunch. Two hours later she brought the same sandwiches home in a crumpled backpack after having identified her son's body at the local hospital. I never used to think about such things in the safety of my own well-crafted routine.

I called Mike and Liz within five minutes of our return from the hospital, my brain addled by shock.

They came straightaway. "The baby will not live," I said the moment they arrived. "It has thanatophoric dysplasia. I can't get through to Paul. I don't know whether I should leave a message on his voice mail? My mom's gone to collect the children. It's Hannah's birthday. What am I going to say to them?"

Others with less wisdom would have filled the place with words, or been drawn into the temptation to give answers and follow wild thoughts in numerous directions, but Mike and Liz waited with me in the shock, allowing the pieces to fall to the ground before identifying which ones needed to be picked up and in what order. Liz wrapped me in a blanket and Mike listened to my broken sentences sifting through the kerfuffle of my anxiety. I expected them to tell me it was wrong to have an abortion; but when they said nothing, despite my questions, I began to relax in their company. When Paul eventually came through the door, they slipped away, but we knew they would come back if we needed them.

Wren had taken the girls straight to a café for a snack. Paul and I were alone. A garbled telephone message had put him in the picture. He looked tired and worn. For a long time we stood in silence with our arms around each other.

The hours that followed are a blur. All I remember is Paul's determination to fend off the shadow that had fallen over Hannah's celebration. "I don't want her birthday to be forever after associated with this. We don't need to tell them until tomorrow." He read the girls a story, we opened presents, and he put them into bed as usual. It's strange how you can do things when you're in shock.

I sat in the living room cuddling my knees. Once I would have been quick to register my opposition to abortion but now I was shocked to find that the only thing I wanted was to get the fetus out of my body as quickly as possible. I wanted this awful pregnancy to be over.

"It's the kindest thing to do, isn't it?" I said as soon as Paul returned, having settled the girls to sleep. As we stared at our dilemma we knew that a stark ethical principle was not enough to carry us through the rest of the pregnancy without hope; it was not enough to enable us to cope with the ongoing nausea, the threat of my back problem, and the chance of watching our baby die in pain. Principles, however sound they might be, were simply not enough to give us the capacity to go on. They stopped short, leaving a great chasm of pain. I remember the desperation in Paul's face as he suggested we pray.

I've often heard people use the phrase "God said to me" but I never understood what it meant until that evening in May when I can only say we felt God speak a message to our hearts as clearly as if he had been talking with us in person. *Here is a sick and dying child. Will you love this child for me?*

The question reframed everything. It was no longer primarily a question of abstract ethical principle but rather the gentle imperative of love. Before we finished praying, the chasm between the principle and the choice had been filled.

As I lay down in my bed that night I realized the decision had been made. I turned in my Bible to the Psalms and read:

Because you are my help,
  I sing in the shadow of your wings.
I cling to you;
    your right hand upholds me.
  (Psalm 63:7–8)

I underlined the words *sing* and *cling,* writing the date in the margin. This is how I would get through the seemingly impossible challenge of the rest of the pregnancy. God would be my help.

4

Sanity

The peace I felt that night did not go away as we returned to
the hospital early the next morning. A large man in his late
fifties greeted me with a broad smile and a firm handshake.
"I hope you slept well, Mrs. Williams."

It seemed a strange comment given the circumstances.
The consultant ushered me into a windowless examination
room, leaving Paul standing bewildered on the threshold.
The consultant parked himself on a stool in front of the
computer. His bulk dwarfed the stool like a parent perched
on a red plastic chair tying their child's shoelace at the end of
preschool. No one addressed Paul and, being unsure of what
to do, he came around the curtain and made for the corner.
When the nurse settled me onto the bed he had to flatten
himself against the wall to avoid her backside. He looked
grim and out of place.

"Now Mrs. Williams – Sarah, if I may. We are going to
repeat the examinations that we carried out yesterday. I'm
going to record some more information and then I will show
you and your husband the findings and we can deal with any
questions you may have."

I put out my hand in an attempt to draw Paul closer so he could at least see the screen.

"Please can you also tell us the sex?" I asked.

"That may or may not be possible. I will see." The consultant bent over the keyboard. The nurse stood behind him with a clipboard while another man, whose identity remained a mystery to us, half lent, half sat on the desk with his arms folded.

I watched Paul's face as our baby appeared on the screen. He was motionless, his eyes riveted to the tiny form, as mine had been the day before. There was movement and life in the figure before us. The doctor spun the cursor from one part of the skeleton to the next, measuring and recording. "The most important feature to note here is the severe global limb shortening. There is also long bone angulation and a marked alteration in bone echo density, all of which point to thanatophoric dysplasia. And there, you see," he continued as if in passing, "even the head is abnormally large as you would expect in these cases. There is likely to be brain damage of course." His voice was unduly loud as if he were speaking to a general audience.

"Thanatophoric dysplasia is best described as a form of severe dwarfism. It is a congenital abnormality, which occurs in about one in seven hundred thousand. Problems in the genetic structure may be inherited from one or both parents, or they may be caused by an initial random error in the arrangement of the chromosomes. I think we're probably looking at the latter here. This particular chromosomal abnormality will result in death either immediately or soon after birth."

"Is the baby in any pain now?" Paul asked.

The consultant carried on speaking for a few moments before he stopped to absorb the question. "That's hard to say. Sometimes the bones break in utero and there is some suggestion that this can cause fetal distress."

"Do you see any evidence of this now?" Paul urged him.

The consultant spent some time reviewing the measurements before he said, "The bones are thin but, no, I can't see signs of fracturing. Fracturing is more often associated with osteogenesis imperfecta type II, and I am 98 percent certain this is a case of thanatophoric dysplasia. No, I do not see evidence of fracturing at present."

"So there is no pain now." Paul turned to me with relief in his voice. "The baby is not in pain now."

"Not now at least," the consultant continued as if to dispel any shred of unreality, "but the pain will come as soon as birth starts. At that point the skeleton will probably be crushed as it moves down the birth canal."

"Is there anything wrong with the heart?" Paul pressed.

"No, not as such. But if you look here you can see there is significant chest compression indicated by a relatively large cardiothoracic ratio. This is consistent with a poor prognosis, but it looks as if the heart itself is OK."

"Did you hear that?" Paul said to me. "There – a healthy heart. There is nothing wrong with the heart."

He was right. The heart pulsated with life.

"And the sex?" Paul asked, not moving his eyes from the screen.

"It is hard to tell in these cases. Sometimes the fetus is androgynous. But it looks female, yes, there you are, female. Although you can never be certain of course, but it does look female."

Paul squeezed my hand almost imperceptibly. "Our daughter," he whispered.

There was something surreal about seeing her there, comfortable, warm, and surrounded by my body, but hearing the doctor's voice in the distance describing her death. I remember thinking distinctly as I watched her: "Hold on a minute, this is her life. She isn't dead. She's alive now. She can hear my heart. She can hear Paul's voice and her sisters' laughter. She can experience different foods as I eat them and most of all she can know the presence of the Holy Spirit while she is in the womb."

"What would a termination involve?" I heard myself say.

"A very simple procedure, Mrs. Williams," the consultant replied. "The normal method is to give an anesthetic and then to inject the fetal heart under ultrasound guidance. Once the fetus is confirmed dead, drugs are then given to induce stillbirth." He paused and looked up at Paul. "Of course you're welcome to a second opinion before making that decision. We can have you examined at Great Ormond Street within a few days." He turned back to me when he saw that Paul did not respond.

"That won't be necessary," I said quietly. "How quickly would I need to decide?"

"Whenever you want to," the consultant said. "You can choose to have a termination right up to thirty-eight weeks' gestation* but obviously you'd want to make the decision as quickly as possible. I will ask my colleague to come in and talk to you further if you wish. She deals more directly with this than I do. My area is really research, which brings me on to another issue. I know it is a little early to be thinking

*In the United Kingdom, the legal limit for an abortion on social grounds was twenty-four weeks, but no restrictions were placed on the termination of babies at any stage in pregnancy in the case of fetal handicap.

about this, but, you will need to think about whether you are willing to grant us permission to do a full postmortem examination on the baby at whatever stage this is relevant. Given the rarity of the disease this would be of great help in research."

"I want to carry the baby to term," I said simply.

The consultant took his glasses off and swung them to and fro between his thumb and forefinger. He did a poor job of masking his surprise. I wondered how many couples rested in his professional medical judgment.

"Well of course there is no pressure to make the decision quickly," he said. "You may need more time to consider. You can come back in a week or a month."

"Thank you," Paul said. "We would like to take some pictures with us if we may. And do you have anything I can read about this condition?"

The nurse shuffled papers on the desk.

"I'm very sorry this child will not live," he said.

I wondered if he thought we were in denial.

"I would find it helpful to read something if I may," Paul continued, "and then we would like to come back and discuss the birth with you." The consultant turned around and said something about a research paper to the unnamed man. He left the room and returned soon after with a ten-page report. "This is about a range of skeletal abnormalities including various kinds of dwarfism so you'll have to wade through it I'm afraid. It's basically an assessment of the diagnostic and prognostic accuracy of sonographic prenatal screening procedures, but I hope it will contain information about the condition that will be of use to you. I suggest you phone my secretary when you're ready to come back and she will arrange an appointment for you. Goodbye, Mrs. Williams."

I think he doubted our sanity when we left the hospital smiling and clutching our baby pictures.

5

Sticky Buns

Emma was angry. She was at our house waiting for the children to come back from school. I knew she was angry because things banged and clattered as she laid the table.

"Shall we go for a quick walk, Emma?" I said.

She looked at the clock. "The girls will be back in five minutes. I haven't finished the tea yet." She wouldn't look at me.

"I'll do it," said Wren emerging from the utility room. "Go," she whispered as Emma went to get her coat, "and don't rush; she needs you."

I'd phoned Emma the night before to tell her about the initial scan. She was distraught and unable to speak for tears but I'd not yet told her about our decision.

We stepped outside. I hadn't even opened my mouth before she launched her tirade. "It's not fair. Not after all that sickness. Why would God let such a thing happen? It's not . . . it's not . . . right."

She shoved her hands deep into her pockets and I was glad it was God she was angry with, not me. "Why did he let you go through all that sickness just for this? You've waited so long. It makes me wonder why we pray!"

I didn't know what to say. I looked at her as we walked along. Her faithful companionship had been firm bedrock for me over the last five and a half years. Her unwavering friendship provided the consistency in our family life and it struck me how characteristically unselfish it was of her to think first of me. We are nearly the same age, Emma and I, but life has taken us down different routes. I have a husband and children, she does not. Paul and I have always known that she loves our children with a strong, protective love that covers over the many irritations that must have arisen from working for us and with us for so long. I found myself saying, "I am sorry, Emma. I know you were looking forward to this baby almost as much as we were."

"Yes, I was." She started to cry. Her abrasiveness had been a smoke screen. It was not just Paul and me who would lose someone precious; Wren would lose a grandchild and Emma would lose someone who would have been as dear to her as Hannah and Emilia.

"Sorry about all the vomiting too," I said.

She cried more loudly, but with a fleeting laugh this time. "It was flipping hard work – all that vomit."

"Thanks for looking after me," I said. "Seems to be the story of our lives, doesn't it?" We both laughed, remembering the days when I would direct Emma, irritable with back pain. Emma's dreams hadn't worked out either and it put things in perspective for me.

We made our way back to the house. "We've decided to carry the baby to term."

"That doesn't surprise me, but how will you cope? What happens if your back goes again? What are you going to say to the girls?"

These questions were not going to go away in one short walk.

"Well, I guess we'll have to cross each bridge when we come to it, won't we?"

"Yes we will." Her voice sounded normal again and I was reassured by the familiar word "we" with all its implications of teamwork. I was glad that we'd weathered a few storms together before this one.

"Thanks for explaining," Emma said as we went through the front door. "It helps."

The girls were leaping around the kitchen, full of the day's events and excited that Wren was still with us.

Paul drew them into the lounge. "Hannah, Emilia, we want to talk to you." His tone stilled their leaping. Wren brought us a tray of tea with some sticky buns. We sat together on the green sofa but we didn't eat the sticky buns.

"Mummy and Daddy have got some bad news. We went to see the doctor and the doctor looked at the baby." Paul was white. I could see how profoundly it pained him to say this to them. I held his hand. "The baby is sick and the doctor thinks she will die when she's born."

He waited, giving them silent space to allow his words to sink in. I would have filled the quiet with words to try and structure their responses, but Paul is wiser than I am.

They both began to cry. "Is the baby alive now?" said Hannah finally.

"Yes, and she is a little girl."

"What is wrong with her, Daddy?" Emilia wailed.

"The bones in her chest are too small and when she's born, she won't be able to breathe."

"Is she in pain, now?" Hannah echoed Paul's earlier question.

"No, she is not in pain now."

After a long pause Hannah asked, "Can we always love her?"

"Yes we can. She's your sister and you can love her now while she's in Mummy's tummy and you can always love her, even after she dies."

Somehow this was enough for Hannah. She wrapped her arms around the bump and cried into my tummy.

But Emilia threw herself against Paul. Gripping his arm she wailed, "I don't want the baby to be sick. I want her to sleep in my bedroom with me."

Paul let her go as she squirmed off his lap and he did not respond as she lurched, catching the corner of the tea tray and spilling its contents.

"I'm going to find Wren," she stormed. "Wren will tell God to make the baby better!"

I knew how Emilia had prayed since she was three for a younger brother or a sister. I looked at Paul helplessly. Hannah wouldn't leave my side even when we moved into the kitchen to pick at the sticky buns.

There were lots of things we might have said to the girls: "Maybe she will get better," or "We'll have another one," or perhaps we could have kept it quiet and only told them at the end. I thought about these scenarios and remembered the time my father didn't tell me how sick my mother really was, and the rage I'd felt toward him when I found out afterward. Paul trades in no other currency but truth and so it did not surprise me that he was direct with the girls, no matter what.

That night we told Mike and Liz of our decision. "We'll support you," they said. "And the church will pray for you."

And I knew they would. Since the pineapple incident, I trusted them.

The next day I phoned Mark and Janet. I'd been putting it off. I could not stop thinking about their baby – their healthy baby. When Josie answered the phone I asked to speak to Mark. I thought it would be easier to say it to him rather than Janet.

"Mark, I had my scan. The baby is deformed. It won't live beyond birth." There was silence, not a word.

"Mark? Are you there? Mark?" All I heard was a strange muffled sound. It was some time before I realized he was crying.

"I am so sorry," he mumbled. "We'll phone you back."

Fifteen minutes later Janet rang. "Can we come over?"

"Yes, of course." But then I hid in the bedroom dreading their arrival. I didn't want to see them. What was I going to say? How would they handle it? How would I feel about seeing Janet in maternity clothes, recalling our last happy, hope-filled conversation? There was no escape. I had to face it.

They stood in the kitchen while I made them a drink. There was an awkward formality that seemed all the more exaggerated by the fact that there had never been any such restraint between us before.

"It's a little girl," I said as we seated ourselves in the lounge. "Paul wants us to name her soon."

They both began to cry. I could not cry. I wanted to but I felt stiff and uncomfortable. I was pushing them away. My eyes looked everywhere in the room but at them.

Janet was sitting next to me on the sofa and she turned around and looked straight at me, brushing her tears to one side.

"Well, I guess we've got a choice, haven't we?"

I'd had my fill of choices lately. I frowned, unsure what she was about to say.

"We can either walk through this together or we can walk through it separately. We can either choose to share the pain together or we can choose not to. We can choose to love one another's babies or we can choose not to."

I was stunned. I could not have taken this kind of directness from anyone else. But I knew exactly what Janet was saying and her bravery in confronting my distance cut right through all the layers of defense and appealed directly to my heart and to the integrity of our friendship. She was not going to pacify me with words to hide the gorge that had opened between us as a result of this news. It was not without reason that I had respected her for so many years.

From that moment on we could talk. She'd broken through the barrier of my silence. I often wonder whether, without the risk she took, we would have been condemned to a friendship of distance and platitudes.

We wove in and out of prayer and conversation – even laughter – for three hours. There were few days that Janet and I did not call each other during that summer and certainly no week went by without journeying through our pregnancies together. Janet chose to grieve with me. Later I would have to choose to celebrate with her. Both choices were costly.

6

Two Big Roads

In the weeks that followed I wished that every relationship could have been as open as this. It was a different scenario with many people at church and at work. I remember watching one person run back into the restroom when she saw me coming. Perhaps she didn't know what to say; but something, even the quickest "I'm sorry," was always better than nothing–nearly always at least.

One lady at church was unwilling to let the matter lie. "You must pray that God will heal this child. Think what a testimony you would have if he did. I'm praying God will do a miracle and heal this baby. It has to be his will to heal." Every time I saw her she said the same thing. She told me about a couple from another church who were fighting cancer. The husband was in the advanced stages of the disease, but still he clung to "his healing." She told me in admiring tones of how he and his wife had traveled the length and breadth of the country and even to South America to be prayed for by various people with healing ministries. She would leave a deliberate pause at the end of her descriptions during which I think I was meant to repent of my own passivity. The one word she never mentioned was death.

After a good six weeks of these conversations I could remain silent no longer. I sat down next to her at the back of church.

"Thank you for praying for our baby," I said. "We need prayer very much, and we really appreciate your concern. I know it may sound strange but I see this pregnancy like two big roads. Each road has a large sign over it. The first one says *Healing* in big letters." I heard her purr next to me at the sound of the word. "The other sign is more difficult to read but I think it says *God Himself.* This path doesn't look nearly so inviting. It's dark and unknown." Nervously, I turned to look at her. "You see, I do not want to spend the precious time I have with the baby searching for healing. I want to spend it seeking God and loving the baby as she is. Paul and I trust that we will find God in the pain, not in the avoidance of it."

I don't think she understood what I was trying to say because she carried on saying the same things to me for the rest of the summer. It was only months later, when the man she'd told me about finally died of cancer, that she began to question if it had really been God's will to heal him. The man's widow was questioning the entire basis of her faith in the wake of his death. If God doesn't heal, perhaps he doesn't love, and if he doesn't love, perhaps he is not good—perhaps he doesn't even exist. This path certainly made the man's last days fraught with tension.

I returned to work a week after we discovered that the baby would die. The college secretary had relayed the news to my colleagues via an official email. The cards I received were precious and I found empathy in unexpected quarters. A senior member of faculty who'd spoken to me only infrequently wrote me a long letter describing how he and his wife had waited for many weeks after discovering that their child was likely to have Down syndrome. When their son was born he was severely handicapped but the letter managed to convey with great simplicity and emotion the supreme delight their son had been to them over the years, not merely in spite of his disability, but also because of it. That letter comforted me.

What I did not anticipate in making the decision not to have an abortion was the anger that it would provoke in some. In one conversation, a university medic presented the moral arguments in favor of abortion in a robust fashion: "To fail to abort in the case of proven fetal abnormality is morally wrong because in doing so one is deliberately and willfully choosing to bring avoidable suffering into the world. It is an ethical imperative to abort in the case of suboptimal life."

I felt like an undergraduate chastised for a weak line of argument in a badly written essay. I knew the argument was not intended rudely or personally – they never are at Oxford – and although I tried only to muse on his argument with the distance of theory, it still kept me awake at night. I knew there was something wrong with the argument. It made me want to ask if he thought the same logic should be applied to the elderly. But I could not, as yet, find a defense, and the force of my colleague's case led me to consider whether I was in fact being selfish in prolonging the baby's life. Being an historian of the nineteenth century, I couldn't help but remember how John Stuart Mill argues against the freedom to reproduce in his essay *On Liberty*. To bring a child into existence without a fair prospect of provision for the body and instruction for the mind, Mill claims, is a moral crime against the unfortunate offspring and against society.

Mill's idea became enshrined in liberal thought, introducing a philosophical case against bringing people into existence under adverse circumstances. But Mill could not have foreseen the arenas in which these ideas would be deployed in the twenty-first century: the wrongful life cases being upheld in Western courts*, the use of utilitarian arguments in the defense of prenatal testing with a view to aborting defective embryos, and the assisted dying debate. The word "suboptimal" rang in my head for days afterward.

Other arguments were both more insidious and more personal. A feminist colleague, whose expertise in linguistics made her a formidable combatant in any discussion, saw me as a traitor to the cause. "Are you sure you're making the right decision?" she said one day on our way to the parking lot. "What if against all the odds the baby should live but be severely mentally and physically handicapped? It will ruin your career, your life. Don't you think it's irresponsible to run that risk? You do have the right to choose, you know."

I was so stunned, I temporarily lost the power of speech. She sidled closer to me and whispered in covert tones, "Is your husband putting you under pressure?"

She'd never met Paul. I nearly laughed.

My colleague said nothing to me for some weeks after that conversation, though I felt her eyes on me every time we passed each other. I thought a great deal about what she said. In many ways I greatly admired her brutal honesty. I thought about what she meant by "the right to choose." What did this

---

*Courts in many US states allow parents to bring action against doctors for "wrongful birth" and a few states allow disabled children to bring action for "wrongful life." The alleged wrong is that the physician failed to diagnose the disability before birth – or failed to adequately inform the parents of the risk of passing on a genetic disease – and is therefore responsible for the birth of an impaired child who would otherwise not have been born and would not have experienced suffering.

phrase mean? As far as I could tell, for her it meant the ability
to practice a principled life of preserving feminine indepen-
dence at the cost of all human intimacy. I spent a long time
thinking what the law really implies when it allows a woman
like me to have an abortion all the way up to full term. What
effect does this law have on a culture? I began to consider
from a Christian perspective what it means to have freedom
to choose. I wrote these words in my journal:

> Rather than being a liberty of autonomy, freedom from
> obligation, or the power to mobilize resources for our own
> ends, liberty is first and foremost freedom from the conse-
> quences of sin and the possibility of enjoying the space to
> choose to serve others and most of all to choose to serve the
> living God. Christian liberty is the Spirit-empowered ability
> to choose to fulfill our obligations, to lay aside comfort for
> the sake of another, and to use all our resources to honor
> and fulfill our created function.

I wished I had the courage to say those words to my
colleague's face.

7

"Suboptimal Life"

I think the phrase goes: "When it rains, it pours." It was the twenty-second of May, nine days after we discovered the baby would die. Emilia had been unwell for some time. She rarely wanted to eat and there was blood in her stool. At first, I put the fatigue down to starting school and the disruption to our normal routine caused by the pregnancy nausea; but when the symptoms worsened and she began to complain of tummy ache, we began to feel concerned.

Hospitals are all too familiar to Emilia. She was born with a malformed windpipe which required surgery at the age of one and a hearing problem necessitated regular hospital visits to fit hearing aids. I had almost forgotten our initial visit to the gastroenterology department when the registrar phoned with the results of Emilia's blood tests, asking us to bring her to the hospital immediately. Paul was inundated with work, having taken the best part of a week off in the immediate wake of the scan, and it was impossible for him to accompany us back to the John Radcliffe Hospital.

Wren drove up from her home in Kent once again. "I'm not leaving you to go into that place on your own after last week's horrors."

"We'll be fine," I insisted "We'll take lots of games to play in the waiting room. She's only having a colonoscopy, after all, and we don't have to go near the women's center. I'll make sure I don't park in the same place so it doesn't remind me of last week."

But Wren came all the same and once again I was glad she was there in the right place at the right time with her quiet prayerfulness. This time she left her laptop at home.

Emilia needed a general anesthetic but they told us she would only be half an hour in the examination room. Wren could see that I was anxious when, after an hour and a half, Emilia had still not emerged from the room where they had taken her on a hospital bed with magic cream on her hands and teddy stuffed under her arm. We chatted too brightly in the waiting room, Wren trying desperately not to let me see that she too was anxious.

When the consultant himself came into the waiting room still wearing his green surgery outfit with flecks of blood still on the cuffs, I nearly collapsed in terror. After the discovery of the previous week, the unexpected and the tragic now seemed plausible.

"Mrs. Williams? I wonder if I might have a word with you, please." I followed him out of the waiting room into a side room.

"Have a seat, would you." He pointed at a plastic chair in the corner. "I'm afraid I have some rather bad news."

I was convinced he was going to tell me she was dead.

"Emilia has severe Crohn's disease. We're going to have to keep her in hospital, I'm afraid, until we can get the disease under control."

The relief was immense. I let out a laugh.

The doctor did not laugh.

Reddening with embarrassment, I tried to explain. "Oh no, I mean . . . we've just had a big shock . . ." But my words trailed away, replaced by a large lump in my throat.

The doctor embarked on this explanation: "Crohn's is an inflammatory bowel disease which in cases as severe as this and so early on in childhood can have long-term implications for growth and development. It is a chronic illness for which there is no cure at present. It's characterized by the inflammation of areas of the digestive tract. Emilia has inflammation throughout her system, causing ulceration and some strictures in the bowel." He continued in a monotone, "It's caused by an overreaction of the body's immune system. No one knows what triggers it off. It could be environment; it could be a genetic susceptibility." He paused for a moment. "She is a very brave little girl. She must have been in a lot of pain. She's not at all well. When she comes around from the anesthetic she's likely to be pretty uncomfortable. I will come and see her when we get you up to the ward."

Wren and I made our way to the children's ward. I kept muttering, "Two daughters. What's going on?"

Emilia lay on the bed looking disarmingly like Paul with her bright eyes and her quizzical expression. She vomited three times as she came around but still she managed to smile. They took us to a small side room on one of the children's wards where they rigged up a drip and began an intensive course of intravenous steroids.

Phoning Paul and then Emma brought back bad memories of the week before. I could hardly believe I was doing it all over again. Paul abandoned his work and caught a taxi straight to the hospital, where he spent an hour questioning the doctor about Crohn's disease. There was something darkly comic about phoning Mike and Liz for the second week running and asking them to pray for us in yet another crisis.

For over a week Paul, Emma, and I took it in turns to sit at Emilia's bedside and sleep on the floor in her hospital room. She charmed every doctor in sight and soon there were nurses in abundance emerging from nowhere to play with her, or to say goodnight before going off duty. Every child in Emilia's class drew a picture and they covered the walls and the windowsill. One of my students even sent her a teddy bear wearing an Oxford University sweatshirt.

Cocooned as I was by the shock of the previous week, it took a while before I took in the implications of Emilia's illness. My mind could not get around the thought of long-term persistent illness and the effort she would face in battling through. It had been hard enough with her hearing problem. As I lay in the hospital beside her, listening to her breathing, and watching the red light on the drip, the word "suboptimal" kept coming back to my mind. Did Crohn's make Emilia suboptimal as well? She would not die of the disease, but where most children would surge across a level playing field in their growth and development Emilia was likely to face an uphill assault course. The doctor laid great stress on lifestyle challenges. He even correlated quality of life with the course of the disease. A long shadow had fallen over Emilia's future. I wondered if, with the rapid development of pre-implantation genetic diagnosis, couples would soon be able to screen and predict the genetic propensity toward autoimmune diseases and in so doing preselect and implant only the healthiest embryos. Why, if this technology is used for serious life-threatening illnesses, should it not also be extended to chronic illness such as Crohn's? Indeed, I had read that the same technologies were being used in some countries to allow parents to choose the gender of the embryo at pre-implantation stage and in some cases to anticipate how likely a baby was to possess certain desirable physical or mental attributes. I recalled how in a recent budget the government had announced their intention to spend 40 million pounds on stem cell research over a three-year period to make Britain one of the leading countries in the world in prenatal research of this kind. I looked around the ward and wondered if such procedures would eventually empty half the beds.

I lay there thinking about these things in the stifling heat of the hospital, exaggerated as it was by the oven effect of pregnancy. I looked at Emilia, remembering the special award she had just won at school for "persistent cheerful-ness." There was nothing suboptimal about her spirit, or the amount of love she drew from our hearts.

Silently, I formed a counterargument against the position adopted by my medical colleague. His argument, along with all the practices I had been pondering, presuppose a partic-ular definition of normality, of health, and of quality of life. But what happens if the definition on which this argument rests is dubious? Whose definition of normality is it anyway? And on what basis is quality of life assessed? What is a normal person? Do normal people have a certain intelligence or skin color? In the 1870s, when John Stuart Mill wrote his treatise, families of twelve regularly lived in one-bedroom cottages with outside toilets. Mill might raise a philosophical eyebrow, but most of the time this was considered perfectly normal. Today, in the Western world, such overcrowding would be considered an intolerable suboptimal cruelty. Surely quality of life is an arbitrary concept. Normality is a relative scale with no accepted criteria in all cultures. At one

end of this relative scale we place people who are restricted
by intellectual functioning, illness, age, or accident. And
at the other end of this scale we place people with efficient
minds and bodies. By this definition each of my three
children sit at different points on the normality spectrum;
but could I as a parent who loves them equally decide which
one of them was most valuable, or worthy of a place on the
planet? Can I as a parent tolerate the idea that Hannah and
my baby in the womb, for instance, are subject to different
legal rights all because of an arbitrary standard of normality?

Later I read the work of theologian Jürgen Moltmann,
who writes:

> In reality there is no such thing as a non-handicapped life;
> only the ideal of health set up by society and the capable
> condemns a certain group of people to be called handi-
> capped. Our society arbitrarily defines health as the capacity
> for work and a capacity for enjoyment, but true health is
> something quite different. True health is the strength to
> live, the strength to suffer, the strength to die. Health is not
> a condition of my body; it is the power of my soul to cope
> with the varying conditions of the body.*

Strangely, it was Hannah, who'd never seen a day's illness
in her life, who struggled most with her sister's illness,
even more so than Emilia did herself. Emilia's humor and
determination carried her through the pain of toilet trips,
the indignity of examinations, and the smarting agony of
repeated injections. But Hannah was tortured by anxiety.
She said very little but her tension was palpable. When she
came to the hospital she sat sullenly kicking the chair. We
could not get her to eat. Finally, after many days, she voiced

* As quoted in Philip Yancey, *Where Is God When It Hurts?* (Grand Rapids, MI: Zondervan, 1977) 190–191.

her fear, just as I walked out of her bedroom after saying goodnight. "Is Emilia going to die too?"

"Oh darling, no, of course not." I returned at once to her bedside, my face close to hers. "Is that what you have been thinking?"

She nodded, hiding her face in the pillow. For days she'd carried this fear unable, or perhaps too timid, to articulate it to anyone. Some people say children are very resilient but I'm not so sure. Children can make connections that adults do not make and, unless we allow them to talk, these connections can get buried, causing untold damage for decades.

"I don't know how to love the baby," I said to Paul that evening. "What can I do for her?"

"How do you think I feel?" he said. "You have her inside you. All I can do is look after *you*."

I had not thought about it like this. *I want to love this baby,* I wrote in my journal, *but I do not know how to.*

I knew how to love Emilia when she was sick and Hannah when she needed to talk; but how should I mother this one whom I may never hold alive? There was an odd comfort in being able to do things for Emilia. The busyness of going to and from the hospital distracted us. I could read to her, I could cut up her food into bite-sized pieces, I could wrap her in a warm towel after her bath in the hospital bathroom. I would never do any of those things for her little sister. When Emilia eventually came home from hospital, we decorated her room with cards and put little treats on her bed. It was a straightforward, tangible kind of loving.

I used to sit on the sofa and gaze at the ultrasound pictures. I was sure I could see her face clearly and I couldn't help but think of the verses I knew so well from Psalm 139:

For you created my inmost being;
  you knit me together in my mother's womb.
I praise you because I am fearfully and wonderfully made;
  your works are wonderful,
  I know that full well.
My frame was not hidden from you
  when I was made in the secret place,
  when I was woven together in the depths of the earth.
Your eyes saw my unformed body;
  all the days ordained for me were written in your book
  before one of them came to be.

As I pondered these verses in June and early July I realized that, if this were true of my child, if God had indeed purposed her and loved her as this passage suggests, then not only did this have profound implications for how I judged "normality" but it also had profound implications for my role as a mother. I began to think long and hard about what it really means to be a mother. I realized increasingly that I wanted this child for myself. I wanted a baby to hold, a toddler to laugh with, a daughter to teach. I wanted to meet my dreams for my family and to fulfill some of my ambitions. I did not want a deformed baby and I certainly did not want a dead one. God began to challenge me: What if his definition of life and health was different from mine? What if this baby's destiny was simply to be with him forever? What if the days ordained for her did not include a birthday? Did it make those days any less precious or meaningful? What if my role as a mother was to cooperate with God's dreams for my child even if they did not fit with mine? If the role I had to play was to help her live life to the full while her short life lasted, and to prepare her for heaven, then for her sake I needed to remain in an intimate place of prayer.

But how can I do this, I wrote in my journal in June, *when I know I am going to lose her? Won't it hurt more if I give my heart away?* Almost at once a verse from Isaiah came to mind: "He grew up before him like a tender shoot" (Isaiah 53:2). I looked up the verse. I knew this passage was talking about the Messiah, who would come into the world as the suffering servant to carry the sin of the world to the cross. But the "him" in this verse was a parent – a parent watching a child grow knowing that child would suffer and ultimately die. God was not asking me to do anything he had not already done himself. It helped me to picture the circle of unbreakable love that exists within and between the persons of the Trinity. I saw myself being drawn into this circle. As a result it became less a question of my loving the baby as me watching God love and then following him in his love.

This image had two profound implications for me. First, I saw how God the Almighty loved with complete self-giving. And second, it took away the dislocation of death. Death would change the way I could share love with my child but it would not take away the love itself. When I saw this, I was no longer afraid to love her and I began to rest with the baby day after day in this interwoven place of love. And I wished I had seen all my relationships like this before, especially when I'd been bereaved in the past. From this perspective death really is more transient than love.

8

Loved One

"We need to give the baby a name," Paul said, and I knew that he too had been thinking about how to love her. That weekend Hannah and Paul scanned every baby name book they could find. They read out name after name, many of them with great hilarity.

"We need a name that expresses her spirit."

Hannah nodded pensively. "Yes, some names tell you what people are like and what they do, but our baby needs a name that says what she means."

Paul and I glanced at each other. This was pretty profound.

"I want something Welsh," Paul said.

I remembered the cold stone, the rain, and the feel of the wind on that Welsh hillside. December seemed so long ago. I groaned – they'd just made the search harder. They worked all day.

The next morning Paul was sitting up in bed when I woke up and I could tell he had been crying.

"I saw the baby in a dream," he said.

Paul doesn't remember dreams very often so I listened intently.

"She was about four years old. Her hair was long and she ran fast through an open field toward the mountains. She was so free." He added quietly, "I feel connected with her now."

He and Hannah continued the search for a name.

"What do you think of this?" He passed me one of the name books.

"Cerian . . ." I read. "How do you pronounce it? With a soft 'c' like certain?"

"No, with a hard 'c' like 'cat.'"

"What does it mean, Daddy?" Hannah asked.

"It's Welsh for 'loved one.' It means 'loved.'" Paul's voice was a bit wobbly.

"Perfect," I whispered.

And so we called her Cerian, and with her name she moved from a future idea to part of us and we began to celebrate her presence. Hannah and Emilia started to address her directly. Hannah would snuggle close and put her arms around my tummy and talk to Cerian when she thought no one else was looking. Emilia bellowed at her sister whenever and wherever she could. We proposed a toast to Cerian at the end-of-term meal. Emilia drew pictures for the baby and Hannah even wrote a song. Paul put his arms around me and the baby at night.

For me worship became an active expression of motherhood. Cerian and I stayed together in a place of intimacy with God day after day, surrounded by prayer. This intimacy was richer than any I had known before. The verse from Psalm 63 became real. I literally *clung* to God because he was *my help* and he enabled me *to sing in the shadow of his wings.* His right hand upheld me. Just as Cerian was totally dependent on me for everything with which to sustain her life, so

I was totally dependent on God for the grace to live through each day and to carry Cerian for him. I was full of peace.

Peace, however, is utterly distinct from ease. Those remaining sixteen weeks of Cerian's life were both the most wonderful and the most awful. For me "the peace that passes all understanding" (Phil. 4:7) was the peace of a lighthouse in the middle of a horrendous storm.

9

The Tape Recorder

"I hate feeling fat. I hate it. I hate it. I hate it." I stomped around our bedroom. "I am not eating any differently and I'm just swelling up. It will take me the rest of my life to lose this much weight. I hate it."

"Well, you are pregnant. People normally get fat when they're pregnant. Isn't that the whole point?" said Paul, not looking up from his book.

"But you don't understand. It's horrible! To be this uncomfortable and for what? Look, even these maternity trousers are tight on me and I am only twenty-eight weeks." Paul sighed and put down his book. How many times had we had this conversation?

"It feels like my body is out of control."

There was a knock at the front door.

"Blast! The midwife's here. She's early. This is not what I need right now. I am *not* in a good place this morning."

"No, I can see that," Paul said.

Hannah and Emilia opened the door to Lois, the Scottish midwife. She came into the hall with her enormous bag.

"Why have you got such a big bag?" Emilia asked. "Do you keep babies in there?"

"No, not babies exactly," said Lois, "but everything to deliver them."

I could see that Emilia was wondering what "deliver" meant and I preempted questions about mailmen by adding, "Lois helps when babies are being born."

"Can you show me what's in your bag?" Emilia persisted.

"I will." Lois followed me into the lounge. She had been thoughtful in arranging to come to our home to carry out the routine prenatal checks. "It will save you looking at all those other pregnant moms, lovie." I was glad of this. A room full of maternity dresses, copies of *Parenthood* magazine, and crawling siblings was my idea of a nightmare. The home visit also allowed the girls to hear the baby's heartbeat and to connect with the developing pregnancy.

"How are you feeling?"

"Fat," I said.

"Hmm . . ." she looked at me. "Yes."

"Great," I muttered under my breath, "I guess I look it as well."

"Can I look in your bag now?" said Emilia.

"Well, as a matter of fact, you can." Lois let Emilia find the blood pressure monitor and she explained to both girls how it worked. After taking my blood pressure she took each of theirs and both girls took her blood pressure in turn.

While she filled out various forms she told the girls of her adventures as a midwife. Their eyes widened as she described the time she was called to a houseboat on the River Thames at two o'clock in the morning. She had to climb across fences and wade through muddy fields before she found the boat.

"Did you have a flashlight?" asked Hannah.

"Yes, I did, but only a small one and I had to carry my bag."

"Wow!" said Emilia, impressed by the sheer size of the bag. "What happened next?"

"They had a dog and it bit me."

"You should always keep dog biscuits in your bag like Wren. Wren's got four dogs but they don't bite."

"Was the baby born?" asked Hannah.

"Oh yes," said Lois, "but we had to light candles so that we could see."

"I definitely want to be a midwife when I grow up," said Emilia, not taking her eyes from Lois's face.

"It was a little boy."

"What did they call him?" Hannah asked.

"Do you know, I can't remember."

Hannah and Emilia occupied themselves thinking of suitable nautical names while Lois examined me. "You are carrying a lot of fluid. A bit too much, I think. When did you last weigh yourself?"

"This morning. I've put on ten pounds in a week."

"Hmm," she mused, still feeling my tummy. "Ten pounds in a week is not good. I think you may have developed polyhydramnios. The baby's deformity may be stopping her from swallowing enough amniotic fluid and consequently your tummy is swelling up."

"... like a hot-air balloon," I added. "That's what it feels like."

"You're likely to go into premature labor at any time. You need to prepare yourself."

I felt as though she had punched me. I had been pacing myself, expecting the pregnancy to last for at least another ten weeks. I had not thought about the end yet. I was only just coming to terms with the beginning.

I lay on the sofa feeling faint while Hannah squeezed vast quantities of green gel onto my tummy ready for the Doppler.

"Now, where's this heartbeat . . . There it is!" cried Lois almost straightaway. "Baby's head is here. This is her back and here is her heart." She turned the monitor right up and the sound filled the room.

Paul stood in the doorway as eager as us to hear the heartbeat.

"She sounds like a horse running," said Emilia.

And she did – just like the wild pounding of hoofs. It was loud, free, and so alive. We listened for a long time. Then Emilia ran upstairs. We thought she might be upset, but then we heard objects crashing around her room and her little legs thumping back down the stairs. "Here we are," she said. "My tape recorder!" She waved her red and white plastic tape recorder at us as she re-emerged.

"What a great idea," we all said at once.

"Yes, it's a great idea," said Lois. "If you want to make memories, make them now." She glanced at Paul.

When the girls had finished helping her put all the objects back into her bag, she sat them down on the sofa next to me.

"Have you two got any questions?"

Silence.

I could see the girls were thinking. Finally Hannah shook her head. "I don't think so."

"Yes, I have a question." Emilia fixed her level gaze on Lois. "Why doesn't Jesus make my baby better?" The atmosphere tensed. Lois looked away. That question obviously had not featured in her training and she shuffled on her heels as she knelt in front of us.

It was Hannah who broke the silence. "That's a good question, Emilia. I would like to know the answer to that question too."

"So would I," I said.

"We all would," Paul added. But we knew there was no easy answer.

Paul took the girls outside to feed the guinea pigs while Lois called the hospital to arrange another scan.

Emilia went to sleep that night listening to her sister's heartbeat over and over again.

10

Awkward Questions

When we arrived at the hospital I was surprised to see that Paul had his briefcase with him. "I have been doing a bit of homework," he said.

It was a different consultant this time. Lean and fiercely intellectual with grey hair and glasses on the end of his nose the consultant shook our hands briefly and stooped over the computer. "My colleague has shown me the images of the last scan. I understand there was some debate as to whether this is an instance of osteogenesis imperfecta type II or thanatophoric dwarfism?"

"The conclusion reached was thanatophoric dysplasia on the grounds that the bone density and the global limb shortening were less consistent with osteogenesis."

I looked at Paul. Where did that come from?

The consultant looked at him too, before he re-engaged with the screen in front of him. He worked silently for some time. We were content to look at Cerian.

His voiced intruded all too quickly. "Yes, Mrs. Williams, you certainly do have polyhydramnios. The uterus is already distended and the fluid levels exceed those expected at twenty-eight weeks. This is a normal corollary of skeletal dysplasia of this kind. Polyhydramnios is one of the most important signs of serious congenital abnormality. Abnormalities make the baby's swallowing mechanism ineffective so that large quantities of liquid accumulate in the amniotic sac. You are likely to go into premature labor at any time."

"And what happens in the meantime?" I said. He didn't seem to understand the question. "Will I just get bigger and bigger?"

"Essentially yes. The uterus will continue to enlarge with the pressure of the amniotic fluid and eventually the pressure will be so great that it will force the uterus into contraction and you will go into labor. You could have an amniocentesis to drain off some of the fluid, but it would need to be done daily in order to keep the levels down."

"And there is some risk to the baby in this procedure." It had been on these grounds that I had resisted the option of having an amniocentesis test earlier in the pregnancy.*

"That is true, although with a fetal condition as serious as this, the situation is somewhat more complex," he replied.

"Does polyhydramnios present any risks for Sarah?" Paul asked.

"Not usually, mainly discomfort. In some very rare cases it is potentially dangerous. Have you thought any more about the question of termination? I would be willing to carry out a termination for you at any point."

There was silence. He busied himself at the keyboard.

I felt scandalized that they were still raising this as an option. I did not trust myself to speak.

---

*Amniocentesis involves the insertion of a hollow needle through the abdominal wall and uterus into the pregnancy sac to allow the removal of amniotic fluid surrounding the baby. Amniocentesis tests are commonly used to detect chromosomal abnormalities such as Down syndrome. In rare cases the procedure can cause miscarriage.

"I read the paper you wrote on prenatal sonographic diagnosis." Paul's voice was calm and measured. "I found it very interesting. What are the statistical chances of the baby living?"

"Approximately 1 percent" said the doctor.

Paul touched my arm lightly. I wondered what couples do when, intimidated by the authority of the white coat and the weighty atmosphere of scientific knowledge, they feel unable to put questions into words. "And by what means are you arriving at that statistic?" Paul asked.

"On the basis of a study of thirty-five cases of skeletal dysplasias considered over a seven-year period from January 1989 to December 1995."

"How many fetuses were terminated within this sample?"

"Termination occurred in twenty-two of the thirty-five cases. Spontaneous abortion or intrauterine death occurred in two cases; there were six infant deaths, and five, that is, 14 percent, of the infants survived the first year."

"How many of those terminated cases would have lived?" Paul persisted.

"That is impossible for us to ascertain other than by forming an opinion as to likely prognosis when a post-mortem examination is permitted."

"So really, you do not have adequate data to make that judgment because 63 percent of women with babies in this condition abort." As an economist, Paul was on home ground with statistics.

"Well . . . Yes," the doctor conceded. "If you put it in those terms, yes."

I could see the men had forgotten me. The consultant was no longer talking to Paul as a patient. He asked him if he was a medical professional.

Paul pressed the point further: "Even if we were to concede that there is a 1 percent chance of survival, let's talk about the 1 percent."

"But . . ." the doctor tried to interject.

"What provision will be made for the 1 percent chance of survival?"

"But this baby will not live." He adopted the same mantra as the previous consultant.

"We have just agreed," said Paul in the same dignified tone, "that there is, even by your statistics, at least a 1 percent chance of survival. Therefore, as a father, it is my responsibility to ensure that all provision is made should that 1 percent chance come about."

"Well, theoretically, yes, but we are talking about a theoretical scenario here." The consultant looked annoyed.

"No, we are not talking about a theoretical scenario; we are talking about my daughter. What will the procedure be if the baby is born and there is a chance that she will survive?"

I groaned. This conversation was beginning to make me panic. I wondered if Paul was in denial. I laid my head back on the pillow while the men talked above me.

Paul continued, "I have spoken to my friend. He is a surgeon at Birmingham Children's Hospital. He has told me of an operation that is done to enlarge the chest cavity. Could this be done in the event of Cerian surviving birth?"

"This procedure would not work in a case of this kind because of the inadequate development of the lungs."

"I wouldn't want any invasive medical intervention," I said, lifting my head from the pillow. "I only want her to be given palliative care, in the room with me so she can die quietly."

The consultant was red in the face. "Mr. and Mrs. Williams, if this theoretical scenario were to take place and the child were to survive for any length of time – which I do not for one minute think will happen – then the decisions that are made regarding the baby's care will not be yours to make."

Paul and I looked at each other, incredulous. This was a red rag to a bull.

"You mean to tell me that we have – or rather Sarah has – the right to decide whether or not to terminate the life of this baby right up to the moment of its birth and yet thereafter we have no rights as parents over the medical care of our child?"

"Of course we would inform you of everything we were doing, but we are legally obliged to do all that we can to sustain the child's life."

"That is a philosophical and a legal contradiction!" said Paul.

"I would not put it in those terms," said the doctor. "There are just two legal systems which operate: one which applies to the mother carrying the unborn child and one which applies to the legal standing of the child after birth."

"That's ridiculous!" Paul was losing it. But the conclusion was plain enough. The unborn child had no legal rights and neither did the parents of a severely disabled child. We were dealing with systemic injustice here but at the time all I could think about was just how large my stomach could get. "What do we do now?" I asked again.

The doctor seemed to have forgotten my existence temporarily. "It is best if you talk to your midwife about that. Technically this is not an obstetric problem. Do you have any other questions?" he said warily.

"No," I glared at Paul. I had to get out of the room. I was going to throw up.

"No," said Paul through his teeth. "We do not have any more questions, for the moment. But we will contact you if we do."

I bolted out of the room.

I could almost see the steam coming out of Paul's ears when he left. "I can't believe it!" he said. "How can something as illogical as that be allowed to happen? I hate this place." So did I, but not for exactly the same reasons.

"Do you really think she may live?" I asked, trying to keep pace with Paul as he stormed to the car.

"No, of course I don't," he blazed.

"Then why on earth did you ask all those questions?" I knew I was playing with fire to try to discuss this when he was in such a state. "It makes me panic when you talk about her living but being so deformed."

"Why does it?" Paul shouted as we climbed into the car. "What would it be like if she lived and she needed care and we were not ready to give it because of some warped research finding by a couple of old men who have spent their life looking at bodies on computer screens. What would I feel like then?"

I was silent.

"Don't tell me what I can and can't ask them. The whole system excludes fathers and it intimidates people and stops them asking awkward questions." He turned on the ignition but made no move to start our journey home. "Just let me love our daughter my way. This is my way of loving her–making sure that we have explored and thought through every option."

I put my head on his hot shoulder. "I'm sorry."

He shrugged, but I wouldn't take my head away. Finally, he put his arm around me. "It is wrong, isn't it?"

"Yes, it is utterly wrong," I said, not sure whether he was talking about the legal system, Cerian's deformity, or life in general. We looked out across the parking lot at the white building with its two entrances, one above and one below.

"In that part they sustain life at all costs," I pointed at the upper end of the building, "and in that part they dispose of babies. If you want a baby but you can't have one you go in that entrance, and if you have a baby but you don't want it you go in up there. In the middle they rob aborted fetuses of cells to help the other lot of would-be parents."

"And there is a different legal code governing both ends and no one ever asks about the contradiction," Paul added. "It's insane. What are we going to do about it?"

"What can we do?" I said.

We drove home two battered idealists feeling tired, sad, and small.

II

The Labor Bag

I tried to pack my labor bag lots of times but I could never quite finish the job. I would lay out my brand new towel and my dressing gown and my carefully selected toiletries and as I did so my thoughts would swing. At one end of the pendulum there was wild hope and anticipation that we might in fact find that the doctors had got it wrong after all and out would come a miraculously healthy little girl. At the other end there was an engulfing terror at the thought of her dead, misshapen body. Then my mind would go blank and I couldn't remember what I had or hadn't packed and I would end up in a heap of desolation.

"How *do* you prepare for a birth and a death at once?" I asked Liz at the end of a morning service in mid-July. "Can anything be more unnatural?"

"We know of some people in Northern Ireland," she replied. "They carried a child to term knowing the baby would die. Would it help to talk to them?"

It seemed a good idea at the time, but Paul and I were nervous as we picked up a telephone handset each. Our trepidation evaporated, however, the moment David picked up the phone.

"I'm glad you called. Tell us about your baby." We were off. It could not have been easier to talk to them and the relief of finding people who understood was immense. Our questions poured out. Most of them – such as, "What happens to the body after we leave the hospital?" or, "Did you take your own blanket for the baby?" – had seemed too detailed and bizarre to ask anyone else. But these details mattered and David and Sally understood exactly why.

"How did you prepare for the birth?" I asked Sally.

"I sewed the baby a little blanket. This helped me anticipate him as a person and it was something to hold on to afterward."

"Did you take pictures?"

"Oh yes, these were so very precious. I had a friend who had a stillbirth right at the last minute. They offered to take pictures at the hospital but she refused. She was so shocked and confused she just wanted to get home as quickly as possible. Afterward she deeply regretted having no image of the baby. At the time she couldn't face holding the baby either and this was a far bigger regret. They let her see the baby two days later in the hospital mortuary but it was not the same and she always felt guilty for not having held the baby close to her. My memory of holding our son is very precious. We took our photographs to a local artist and from the face he drew a wonderful charcoal etching of the baby. It is in our lounge. We also took a lock of hair and we had a footprint made with a mold."

"What was it like watching the baby die?"

"Terrible, but also beautiful in a strange sort of way. He lived for nine hours. I held him in my arms and told him how much I loved him and what I would have liked to do with him if I'd had the chance."

"And the deformity?" Mike and Liz had already explained to us that their child had died of a structural abnormality called anencephaly. The baby had been born without the upper part of the brain; a large part of the lower brain and the flat bones of the skull were also missing. I was afraid to ask this question and my heart raced.

"It's important," Sally said slowly, "to let yourself explore their deformity. It leaves no room for fear to grow and afterward you may always wonder and wish you had. For us the imagined appearance was actually much worse than the reality."

"How did your other three children grieve?"

"Differently. There is no mold. The older one showed a lot of emotion at the time and the younger one none at all. The middle one just kept on asking questions until we were weary of it. It takes time for them, and the important thing is to let them do it their way."

"Did they come to the hospital and see the baby?"

"Oh yes. That was vital, although it was important to prepare them well beforehand. In order to avoid unnecessary distress the staff wrapped the baby in a blanket so all they could see was the face. They needed to say goodbye to their brother and to let him go. It seemed more painful at the time but in the long run it was much better for them."

"What was it like for you, David, watching the labor?" Paul asked. His voice sounded distant even though he was only sitting upstairs in the study using the other phone.

"Hard," David said. "I felt helpless. It was not until the baby was born that I really bonded with him. It's hard when you're a guy; you don't get to know them like the mom does. And then he was gone too soon. You kind of distance yourself before the birth. You have to in order to survive, I guess, but then when he was there in my arms there wasn't any distance to protect me anymore and the grief kind of hit me. Afterward, people kept asking me, 'How's Sally? Is she okay? How are the kids? Sally must be feeling dreadful?' No one ever asked me how I was or how I was feeling. I was pastoring the church at the time and I felt like I had to say all the right things to people, but inside I felt like punching them and shouting at them, 'Can't you see I am hurting too?'"

After an hour and a half we started to say our goodbyes, and within twenty minutes of the call I had packed my labor bag, fortified by the sense of companionship.

12

An Angel in Yorkshire

"What am I meant to do now?" I wailed at Paul on the last day of the children's school term. I had packed my bag thanks to David and Sally and we had written a birth plan in case I went into labor. Even the car parking money was in my purse, and the numbers to call for prayer and to notify people after the birth were in a prominent place on the pinboard in the kitchen. The university term had finished, finals results were out, and I was officially on maternity leave. There was nothing left but the suspended animation of anticipation and dread.

"Do we just sit around and wait for the baby to come? Do we go on holiday? Do we stay here? Each day I wake up and I don't know if it will be today, tomorrow, or two months' time. I don't know how to plan, how to shop, how to respond to invitations. I don't even know how to dress." The last days of my pregnancies with Hannah and Emilia had felt like months and the agonizing state of limbo I was experiencing this time could in reality continue for another eight to ten weeks.

Paul nodded pensively. "Fun!" he said suddenly. "That is what we need. Something that will be relaxing for us and fun for the girls."

Fun was not a word which I could in any way associate with the rack-like tension I was experiencing. "And where exactly are we going to find that?"

"No! You can't be serious?" said Emma when Paul told her later that day that we had decided to go camping with the whole church in Yorkshire. "What will Sarah sleep on? She can barely sleep in her own bed, let alone the floor of a tent."

"Well, it won't make much difference then, will it?" Paul grinned at her. "It's me you should be worrying about, Emma."

"What happens if Sarah goes into labor at the camp?"

"There's a hospital in Harrogate. And my rally driving techniques are superb, as you know." Emma looked at him doubtfully. "I've called them," he added. "I even got through to the maternity ward. They were very friendly."

Emma scowled.

"The children will have something fun to do," I said, trying to add a touch of practicality to the reasoning.

"They will love it." Paul's enthusiasm grew with Emma's agitation. "All their friends will be there. There are children's groups for them. Mark and Janet are going. Come on Emma. It will be fun."

Emma shook her head. "I've heard that one before. Insanity, that's what it is – pure insanity."

I had used the same word in earlier discussions that day, but now I was hurling myself at the idea with abandon. After all, the probability of insanity was high either way. Staying home I would go insane, and in going I would at least stand a chance of going insane with a degree of hilarity.

"Well," Emma said at last, "I guess I could bring my one-man tent and put it up next to yours. . . . You may need a bit of extra help." We all laughed and the girls cheered and danced in delight at the prospect.

The next few days I almost forgot the shadow of future events in the upheaval of organizing camping stuff, packing saucepans, and cleaning sleeping bags. Paul had wild ideas of taking a portable camping fridge, heater, and barbecue, but he was at work and so Emma and I cleaned the grill, searched for utensils in the attic, and shopped for waterproof matches and tent pegs. It would be more precise, in fact, to say that Emma did the work because she kept on insisting that I rest, yelling at me when I attempted to climb the stepladder into the attic. "Don't even think about it. You are *not* going up there. You won't even fit through the hatch." This last comment at least made me hesitate. "Insanity, that's what it is, utter insanity. For goodness' sake, go and lie down!"

The car was full to overflowing. Our car is affectionately known as Rocket, or less affectionately by Paul as "the West Wing"—it is, after all, slightly bigger than his study! It is a seven-seater which, as I recalled when the last few bits were crammed onto the back seat, we had bought in anticipation of more children. I sighed and leaned against the door. Plans . . . perhaps I should give up making them.

"Look," I said to Emma as we finally shut the front door ready to leave. I held up a small pocket-sized first aid pack. "If anything goes wrong, at least we're prepared!"

She roared with laughter. "Fat lot of good that will do us."

And so we set off with a great feeling of irresponsible freedom. By the time we reached North Yorkshire, Paul had finished his last work call and the phone was ceremonially shut down.

"We're on holiday!" he proclaimed to the motorway.

Mark and Janet arrived before us. Their pitch was comfortably close and all five girls disappeared on their bikes with much merriment. After helping Paul and me unpack our belongings, Emma erected her little yellow tent. Paul made the first cup of tea, and we gazed at the prospect of a happy week.

Janet was forced to use crutches because she had developed painful symphysis pubis dysfunction caused by the instability of the pelvis during pregnancy. We both rejected the hard-backed seats after the first prayer meeting and Mark and Paul carried our comfortable sun loungers into the auditorium and parked them next to each other near the front. Janet and I moved so slowly that we would barely make it back to the tent before it was time to set off for the next Bible study.

It was hot, and for the pregnant it was unbearably hot. Janet and I sat outside our tents fanning ourselves with programs while Paul and the children had long and messy water fights. The worst moment for Emma and me came when – in order to exact revenge for a dastardly act during a previous water fight – a youth worker burst into our tent and tipped an entire dishpan over Paul's head.

"That's the end of water fights!" said Emma categorically.

The children threw themselves into their "big groups" with much enthusiasm. Between meetings they roamed the campsite on their bikes with their friends, returning only to hear Paul read the next chapter of *The Hobbit* at bedtime.

And then, half way through the week, it began to rain. It did not stop for two days. The days of Noah seemed to be upon us again. Tents flooded and caravans leaked, awnings were washed away and wellington boots filled up with water.

People abandoned the camp in droves, some seeking shelter in nearby hotels and others just making a beeline for home.

"You call this fun!" Emma remarked as we trudged back from the toilet block feeling very little difference between the downpour and the cold shower we had just queued half an hour for.

"Well, on a relative scale this could be called a comparatively light and momentary affliction, don't you think?" I was rather enjoying the spectacle of near hysteria and despair that we witnessed inside every other tent. To our amazement our tent did not flood and neither did Emma's. We felt like the Israelites watching the Red Sea close over the Egyptians after they had walked through on dry ground – relieved, triumphant, but a tad guilty too. Although we had no dry garments left, we did not fare too badly, and good humor did not fail us.

In fact, the deluge itself became a place of encounter, particularly for Emilia. Hannah, Josie, Becky, and Mary burst into the tent just as the lightning cut across the sky for a second time. They counted three between the ominous rumblings of thunder and the next clap of lightning.

"Where's Emilia?" I asked, handing them a mug of hot chocolate. They looked at each other blankly.

"I thought she was following us," said Josie.

"So did I," said Hannah.

"Where were you?"

"We were down at the bottom of the field by the big gate that doesn't open. The thunder started and we all got scared so we came back."

"But not Emilia?"

"We thought she was with us."

I resisted the temptation to berate them. They knew only too well that Emilia did not move as quickly as they did. I saved the irritation for myself and the incapacitation that prevented me from walking down the hill, let alone back up again. Emma and Paul put on their boots.

"You stay here with the girls," they said. They pulled back the tent flap and dived into the rain. I tried not to look worried.

The gate marked the furthest point of the campsite. It was some distance from any of the tents. Emilia's little legs would not have carried her up the hill at the pace of the others and I knew she was frightened of thunder.

Eventually, Paul returned with Emilia on his shoulders. Emma followed behind, dragging the bike up the hill. The gaps between the thunder and the lightning were lengthening but still the storm prevailed and it was almost dark at four in the afternoon. Paul put the freezing child down on my lap. I wrapped my arms around her, feeling the sodden deposit of her wet clothes though layers of jumper and maternity trousers.

"Have some hot chocolate. It will warm you up." Paul handed her a large chunk of Cadbury's Dairy Milk to dip into her drink. "She was very intrepid," he said. "Tell Mummy about your great adventure." Emilia polished off the chocolate before she would speak.

"There was a big storm," she began.

"I know darling. I could hear it. It was so loud."

"Hannah left me behind and I was all alone. I was very frightened. I thought I might get struck by lightning if I went on my bike and I couldn't remember which way to go back."

"So what did you do?" I asked and hugged her tightly,

feeling a wretchedly neglectful mother letting my sick five-year-old child roam the campsite alone.

"I sat down and curled up in a ball and I cried. But then I saw an angel and I wasn't frightened anymore. I just waited there until Daddy came and got me."

"An angel?"

"Yes, an angel." She sipped her hot chocolate.

"What did it look like?" I asked.

"Like a normal angel, of course."

I didn't want to sound ignorant of such things, but I couldn't stop myself asking, "What does a normal angel look like? How did you know he was an angel, Emilia?"

"He smiled at me and I felt all warm and I didn't feel frightened anymore. I knew he was an angel." She spoke with a simple nonchalance that made me feel cumbersome in my adult sophistication.

"Have you seen angels before, then?" I asked.

"Of course I have," she said, looking at me as if it were an odd question, "when I was at the hospital and my tummy hurt. They are always looking after me. Can I go and play with Becky now?" She slipped off my lap, put her boots back on, and ran out into the storm to find Mark and Janet's caravan. Paul and I stared at each other dumbfounded and we prayed for childlikeness to meet our storm with faith.

On the final and wettest morning of the camp the speaker took his text from Psalm 22:

> My God, my God, why have you forsaken me?
>> Why are you so far from saving me,
>> so far from my cries of anguish?
> My God, I cry out by day, but you do not answer,
>> by night, but I find no rest.

Yet you are enthroned as the Holy One;
  you are the one Israel praises.
In you our ancestors put their trust;
  they trusted and you delivered them.
To you they cried out and were saved;
  in you they trusted and were not put to shame. . . .

But You, Lord, do not be far from me.
  You are my strength; come quickly to help me.

The speaker described a king on a cross. He spoke of the
glory of God revealed in and through suffering and he
spoke of the strength of this king manifest through ultimate
weakness and vulnerability. There is room, he said, for us
to lament before God. "In fact we need to learn to lament.
Have we got room in our understanding of God for his
apparent absence – and the maturity that comes from
continuing to trust him anyway? The cross was the place of
Jesus' enthronement. If Jesus is our master then should we
not also expect to face suffering? But if we trust God in our
frailty we too are vindicated as Jesus was ultimately."

I sat still at the end of the talk for a long time. When I
began to weep, I let my long hair fall over my face so that
people would not see my tears. I wanted to be alone to think.
My tears were not just of sadness; they were also tinged with
relief – relief that the message provided me with a theological
structure through which I was able to meditate and interpret
my experience. During the time of worship which followed
a very clear picture came into my mind. I saw a rider on
a great black stallion charging toward me with force and
haste. *I am coming to deliver you.* The words impressed themselves on my heart. I tried to draw the image in my journal
but failed and resorted to words instead. Both the talk and

the image meant a great deal to me at the time, but I had little idea then just how important they would be later.

We survived the deluge, but by the time I sank into a hot bath at home the thought of more "fun" had lost its attraction. We were glad to be home. Another week had passed. Thirty weeks, I thought, looking at my tummy protruding above the surface of the bath water. Who would have thought it? I heard the phone ringing in the distance. Hannah brought me the handset. It was Wren: "Why don't you come down here for the rest of the summer? Paul can commute to London from Hildenborough station."

"Really? Are you sure we won't overwhelm you?"

"Isn't that what grandmothers are for?" I climbed out of the bath, repacked, and we set off again, this time to Wren's house in Kent.

13

The Cerian Summer

Everything in Wren's house is conducive to peace. She opens
her home to individuals, groups, and churches for "Quiet
Days," and over the years the building itself has adapted to a
pattern of hospitality. At the side of the house there is a room
dedicated to prayer. There is a cross on the bureau forming
a focal point and a beautifully formed figure of Christ on the
cross wearing a crown of thorns which my brother Justyn
made for Wren as a gift. The chairs are comfortable. Music
is always to hand, as are tissues, and warm fleece blankets to
curl up under. Two full walls of the prayer room are glass.
They are covered in part with well-tended houseplants but as
you look through them there are views on both sides. In the
summer the windows are usually open and you can feel the
breeze and smell the fragrance of the garden.

I know of no other garden as full of flowers as Wren's. In
amongst the flowers there are interesting places to sit. There
are statues, a pagoda, and a huge swing, which Wren seems
to use as much as the grandchildren, and a wooden chalet
filled to overflowing with readily accessible art materials.
Beyond the trees at the bottom of the lawn is a wooded
area where if you look carefully you can just make out the

children's camp. Further on there is another more secret garden and from there the path winds down through the orchard to the woods. The four dogs usually show people the way.

After dropping Paul off at the sleepy local railway station, I used to sit most days in the prayer room, reading my Bible and listening to music. The girls never grew tired of the backyard. They made a bivouac in the woods and created fairy castles in the roots of the trees. Paul made them a see-saw and from there they carried out adventures to the islands in the middle of the pond. The midsummer midges were unbearable but the girls didn't seem to notice. They improved the tree house and swam in a huge paddling pool borrowed from Wren's friend. When the girls grew tired of it, Wren slipped out and bought a slide to which she attached a hose so the girls could hurl themselves down into the pool at high speed.

Wren set a hammock up on the lawn under the shade of the largest oak tree and I often sat there in the afternoons. When Paul came home in the evenings we would sit on the terrace and eat our supper together as it grew cool and dark in the backyard.

Wren canceled all her engagements so she could be at home with us weaving this environment of peace. Each day she took the girls for walks with the dogs across the surrounding countryside. Emilia found a hiding tree and jumped out at people as they walked past. I tried to accompany Wren, dogs, and children on these walks but as my tummy grew I could soon only go as far as the lane. On one of these walks a car approached just as we turned into the lane.

"Car!" Wren called, pulling the dogs on the lead to restrain them.

"Watch out, girls," I called.

In a flash, Emilia rushed into the road, came up behind me, and pushed me with all her strength into the ditch, throwing herself in behind.

"What on earth did you do that for, Emilia?" I exclaimed when the car had passed.

"Because I thought you were going to die. You might have been squished by the car."

"I think it is more likely the car would have been squished by me." It took both girls and Wren to pull me out of the ditch. It was a curious thing for Emilia to do and I couldn't shake off the disquieting sense of foreboding that it left with me.

By the end of August it was too painful to walk. One afternoon on my drive to collect Paul from the station I stopped to tank up the car. I was having a happy day until then. The cashier took my card. Her eyes slid from my face to the bump. "You're huge," she said. "Are you having twins?"

"No," I muttered grimly, "I am not." And I didn't tell her I was still only thirty-two weeks. I walked out without saying thank you.

After we'd been at Wren's house for three weeks Emma arrived. She quickly blended into the quiet rhythm of the summer. She too sensed the safety of that prayer-filled place.

Sunday by Sunday we had our own services in the prayer room. I couldn't face meeting strangers at Wren's church who invariably smiled excitedly at the bump and asked me about the due date. Our little family services were precious times. We each brought a reading or a song, a piece of artwork or a prayer. On one occasion Hannah read the words from Revelation 21 that she copied into her journal:

> Then I saw "a new heaven and a new earth," for the first heaven had passed away, and there was no longer any sea. I saw the Holy City, the new Jerusalem, coming down out of heaven from God, prepared as a bride beautifully dressed for her husband. And I heard a loud voice from the throne saying, "Look! God's dwelling place is now among the people, and he will dwell with them. They will be his people, and God himself will be with them and be their God. 'He will wipe every tear from their eyes. There will be no more death' or mourning or crying or pain, for the old order of things has passed away."

Emilia did an obscure drama at one point in which I died, went to heaven, and then came back again! We laughed at the time but I could not help connecting her sketch with the ditch escapade.

We spent many hours talking in different configurations. Hannah sat next to me on the hammock and sewed a delicate pair of booties for Cerian. She was proud of her work and I could barely look as she sewed the final touch, two tiny pink roses on either toe. Wren also tried to make something for the baby but the shawl she was crocheting would not turn out as she had pictured. In the end she threw her efforts down in disgust and went to Tunbridge Wells and bought a shawl as light and delicate as a spider's web. I molded a cross from clay in the craft room and Emilia spent all her savings on a tiny bright yellow dress that she caught sight of in a shop window. When Emma arrived she brought with her a beautiful cotton quilt made by her mother with Cerian's initials embroidered on the corner. She also handed me a small tissue paper package.

"I've been keeping this in my bottom drawer. It doesn't look like I'll be needing it." She said. "I want Cerian to have it."

I opened the tissue paper. Inside was a handsewn cotton bonnet of the kind that I associate with the late nineteenth century. It was exquisite.

"Thank you," I said. It was all I could say, but I knew how much it meant for her to give me this.

Afterward, Wren remarked that one of the things she was grateful to Cerian for was the long summer we all spent together. Our memories are crammed full of beautiful things. On the tenth of August I wrote in my journal: *What can I do but press on to hear the voice of God and listen to every intonation of his heart? I will press on to appreciate what is beautiful and do what is lovely.* Wren helped me to do these things.

It is strange how one can operate on two levels, particularly in times of grief. I was calm, even placid, on the outside, but inside I was in a turmoil of agony. I could not bear to part with Cerian. I had given her my heart. The polyhydramnios was becoming increasingly painful. My stomach was tender to the touch. I needed help to get out of a chair. I could not sleep for more than forty-five minutes at a stretch either day or night, finding it impossible to get into a position that brought relief from the pain. From four in the afternoon the nausea was unbearable and I would pace around the house not knowing what to do with myself. My back began to hurt very badly. When I slept I dreamt, anticipating Cerian's death through vivid and troubling images. I had to fight to stay calm some days, actively putting my trust in God. One whole page of my journal is covered with these words: *Even though I walk through the valley of the shadow of death I will fear no evil* – the *will* is heavily underlined – *because your rod and staff they comfort me.* I prayed that Jesus the Good Shepherd would walk with me through this dark and frightening valley.

On the next page of my journal I glued in the quote: "Courage is not the absence of fear and despair; it is the capacity to move forward confidently trusting the maker of the heavens to cover us with the shadow of his mighty hand even if the sky should fall."

Soon after we'd arrived at Wren's house I'd been to see the local doctor. I had to register at the nearby health practice and with Pembury Hospital in case the baby should be born. Wren dropped me off at the surgery on the way to the swimming pool with the girls. I had barely begun to read the magazine article in front of me when my name appeared on the screen above me.

I was startled and disarmed when the first question the doctor asked me as I walked into her office was: "Did you decide not to have a termination on strong religious grounds?"

There was something in the manner of the question that made me hesitate. I sensed she wanted an explanation in order to compartmentalize my decision and so to shut it down.

"I do have strong religious beliefs," I said after a pause, "but I'm not sure that's the reason I decided not to have a termination." She turned to face me and raised an eyebrow.

I thought to myself: *Cerian is not a strong religious principle or a rule that compels me to make hard and fast ethical decisions. She is a beautiful person who is teaching me to love the vulnerable, treasure the unlovely, and face fear with dignity and hope.*

"How can a person grieve a termination?" I said simply.
"This baby is alive now and I want to welcome her into our
family. This may be all the time I will get with her and I
want to spend it well. When she dies I will have the comfort
of knowing that I did my best for her and I left God to decide
the rest." I couldn't believe I was saying these things to a
total stranger.

The doctor looked down at my notes. "What have you
told your other children?" She didn't look at me but I knew
she was paying careful attention.

"We told our children the truth, the medical truth, that
they're going to lose her. They helped us give her a name
and they love her." This was not my normal conversation
with doctors. I was expecting her to start shuffling papers
and drawing the meeting to a close even though I hadn't yet
told her why I'd come. But she kept on asking questions.

"What have you named her?"

"Cerian," I said.

"That is an unusual name. I have not heard it before."

"It means loved one. We wanted to choose something
unique because she is a unique person, whatever happens to
her."

To my extreme embarrassment the doctor began to cry.

"What a beautiful attitude toward people," she sniffed. "I
think you should write a book about this one day."

It was time to start talking about my back. This meeting
was getting very intense. "To be honest, I have come not
only to register but to say that I am terrified of having an
epidural because of my back problem, but I am wondering if
my back will cope with labor if I do not."

She blew her nose. "I will arrange for you to go and talk to the consultant anesthetist at Pembury Hospital. He will talk you through the options."

I thanked her and left the surgery in some haste. What an extraordinary conversation! And her response intrigued me: "a beautiful attitude toward people." The connection she'd made fascinated me and I started to think about how our treatment of the weak tells a great deal about the attitude of society toward people in general. Perhaps, in a culture which disposes of the abnormal and weak, the choice not to have a termination does need an explanation.

14

Thai Green Curry

My journal entries for August 24 and 25 are not a happy read:

I despaired last night. Every day she grows inside me.
Each day it hurts my back but how much more it hurts my
heart. Every day I love her more. In one moment I want the
physical pain to end and for the delivery to happen and then
in the next I pray for just one more day with her. I can't go
on like this.

My brain is pulverized. I can't pray any more. I asked God
to take the nausea away but he didn't answer my prayer. I
asked God for mercy in letting her come prematurely and
I have been waiting every day since early July. I asked God
to take the back pain away but the more I pray the worse
it gets. In January I even asked him for an easy pregnancy.
With this track record how can I trust him with the labor?
I pray abstract prayers about his presence but I find it hard
to really trust him to be good to me in the detail. My faith
and trust are stretched to the limit. I am angry with you,
God. The sheer physical discomfort is making me cross and
I am wearied by the never-ending nausea. I can't be positive
anymore.

P.S. Please help me!

I abandoned my journal in the prayer room, and walked into the kitchen. "Mum, I can't go on like this much longer."

"I know," she said. "It's hideous. I can't bear it for you." She turned from putting the kettle on to peer at me. "Are you feeling all right, darling?"

This seemed a strange question. Of course, I did not feel all right, but I felt no worse than normal. "What do you mean?"

"You are . . . you are . . ." She came over and turned my face to the window. "You are blue. I don't like the look of you. I think we should call the doctor."

"I'm fine. I just feel fed up and a bit faint, that's all." I sat down at the kitchen table. "I have a specialist appointment with the anesthetist at Pembury tomorrow. They'll check me out then."

"I don't like the look of you," Wren repeated. "I will take you tomorrow. Emma has already said she'll look after the girls. Paul's in London again tomorrow, isn't he?"

"Yes. Where is he now, by the way?"

Paul was fixing the girls' bikes. They were planning a major bike ride for that afternoon.

I went out to the drive to find him.

"Hello!" Paul greeted me, looking up from the bike pump. "I've booked a Thai restaurant in Sevenoaks for tonight. We all need a bit of a treat and it's a good way to say thanks to your mom for having us here for so long. We'll have to go home to Oxford on Saturday." It was now Tuesday. I was all too aware that our time was nearly over.

"That sounds good." I stood still. I was feeling decidedly faint.

"Are you all right?" said Paul. "You look a bit blue. I'll get you a chair."

84

By the evening I'd recovered a little. I washed my hair and put on my favorite maternity smock. A large ornamental fish pond lay just inside the entrance of the restaurant, and a model waterfall cascaded down a channel to one side of the staircase. Emilia's best dress was drenched in seconds. And Paul nearly impaled a tropical fish with the car keys as he tried to wrestle Emilia's arms out of the tank. Hannah walked ahead demurely, pretending she didn't know the rabble in the doorway.

The sodden dress was forgotten, however, as soon as the meal arrived. We were all absorbed in attending to a choking fit that overtook Emilia as soon as she swallowed her very first mouthful of Thai green curry. Hannah, the traditionally less adventurous of the two when it came to food, quietly chomped her way through three courses. In between frequent toilet trips to deal with wet dresses, rejected curry, and Crohn's symptoms, we proposed toasts to Wren. We each took it in turns to describe one thing we were grateful to Cerian for. Wren talked about the Cerian Summer. Emilia said how grateful she was that Cerian was now the youngest in the family, not her. Emma described how Cerian had made her want to learn more about God. I wrote these memories down at the back of my journal on what I called the "goodness pages." I didn't realize as we left the restaurant that this was the last time that the seven of us would be together.

15

Cold Tea

I knew Pembury Hospital from my childhood. I had spent a week there when I was eight suffering from a rheumatic virus. Wren had given birth to two of her children in the labor ward and all three of my brothers played rugby, so we had often been back with various broken bones. As we drove into the hospital parking lot I wedged my hot Starbucks tea into the container by the glove compartment. "I'll drink that when we get back. This should only take a few minutes."

"Good idea," said Wren.

The waiting room was full of pregnant women. I thought they ought to have looked happier than they actually did. I could not take my eyes off them, thinking of all the joy of anticipation and the well-prepared nurseries.

"Mrs. Williams? Do come this way. . . . You're a new patient? From Oxford? Is this your first visit to Pembury?" The nurse chatted all the way down the corridor to the consultant's room. "The doctor's very nice; you'll like him. Don't worry, he knows all about your little one. I made sure he had the notes in advance." I thanked her profusely.

The doctor invited me in. I told him about my long-standing terror of epidurals and the nature of my back problem. He drew a diagram of the spine and showed me how they would inject the epidural into the spinal column above the injury in the disc between L4 and L5. At first I thought it was the diagram and the talk of injections that was making me feel hot and dizzy. But when my eyes started to fill with bright shiny stars and the desk seemed to move around the room in front of me and three identical doctors talked to me at once, I began to think that perhaps something was wrong. I lowered my head onto my chest. The doctor carried on speaking.

I felt decidedly strange as I made my uneasy way back down the corridor leaning my hand on the cold wall for support. Wren took one look at me and jumped up. I managed to say, "I'm not feeling well," but I couldn't keep my eyes open properly. Wren beckoned to the nurse and together they guided me to the sofa. I closed my eyes. The whole room was spinning now. I just caught a glimpse of another nurse bring over a blood pressure monitor.

"Her blood pressure is very low. I think we should get her down to the labor suite and get one of the doctors to look at her."

I remember being pushed in a wheelchair and taking large gulps of fresh air in the hope they would wake me up. I held the metal armrests tightly. We were greeted by a senior midwife called Marilyn. I remembered her name distinctly through the spinning because she said it so loudly. I sensed her pristine efficiency disorientating Wren.

"This sounds like an anxiety-induced migraine to me," she said, as she and another nurse helped me onto the bed. "Nothing to worry about at all. Let me take your blood pressure. What was it when you took it?" she asked the nurse who had brought me down to the labor suite. Marilyn

pinched my arm into the black canvas band with a rip of
Velcro. She went quiet and her previous manner gave way
to swift professionalism. "Call a doctor . . . immediately. We
need a drip here. Her blood pressure is too low and it is still
falling. Emergency equipment please . . ."

The last thing I heard her say was, "Where is her
husband? We need to contact her husband." She raised her
voice and called across the room, "Can someone call her
husband please. He needs to come immediately."

I tried to say, "Please, get Paul" to Wren but she was
scrabbling in her handbag trying to find his mobile number.
The oxygen mask was over my face by then and she couldn't
hear me. I was aware that they were taking her out of the
room. I tried to call her but I couldn't keep my eyes open
anymore. I heard someone shouting at me from behind,
"Stay with me, Sarah, stay with me. Try to concentrate
on staying awake." The staff were moving me. We were
moving fast down the corridor. People swarmed around me
from all directions, pushing equipment. I saw Wren standing
with a nurse. They were trying to make her sit down. I tried
to speak to her but I was drifting off again. But I couldn't
open my eyes anymore. I wanted Paul to be there.

The bed stopped but I was still moving. I was going up.
I was up above them all looking down at myself. There
were people all around my body. It didn't look like me. Still
they were running. They were wrapping me in a large foil
blanket. There were electrodes all over my chest. They were
scanning my stomach. Someone was shouting at me again,
but I couldn't hear them. Everything was quiet in my head
now. I was drifting again. I could feel the presence of God,
or maybe it was unconsciousness? Whatever it was, it did not

hurt and I felt full of peace. *Am I dying?* I thought. *Well, this is not so bad. It doesn't hurt.*

Then nothing.

Later Wren described how she'd run outside the building to use her mobile phone. She couldn't find Paul's number and so she called Emma at home. Emma was in the yard playing with the girls when the phone rang. At first she thought she'd let it ring on to the answer machine but glancing at her watch she decided it could be Wren apologizing that she was late.

"Emma? We need to get an urgent message through to Paul. Can you do that for me?"

The tension in Wren's voice made Emma clutch the back of the chair. "Of course," she said. This did not sound like the onset of labor. "His office number is written out on the piece of paper above my desk. Can you see it?"

"Yes, I have it." Emma's hands were shaking.

"Sarah's collapsed. They think the baby is pressing on a main blood vessel. They've rushed her into the high dependency unit. The hospital needs him to get here as fast as he can. Things are not looking good."

While Emma waited for the secretary to answer the office phone she looked across the garden at the children. They were taking it in turns to crash at high speed down the slide and into the pool, oblivious of all but their game. Emma felt sick. How was she going to get through this day giving nothing away? Having left the message, she took a deep breath, closed her eyes and prayed. God and sheer professionalism carried her through the afternoon. She played with the girls. She walked the dogs, administered Emilia's medication, cooked supper, bathed the children, and read them bedtime stories before she heard any further news.

As soon as Wren had finished the call she ran back to find me, but they wouldn't let her into the room. The nurse was kind but firm. She made Wren sit outside in the corridor. She kept patting Wren's shoulder and murmuring calming words but giving away no information. All Wren could see were people running in from different directions, looking grave and wheeling equipment. She thought she was losing me. She prayed that Paul would get there quick.

Paul was in a meeting in London. It was unusual for meetings to be interrupted and the assembled crew looked up in surprise when Paul's personal assistant knocked and walked in. "Excuse me, Paul. I have an urgent message for you from Pembury Hospital."

"Is she in labor?" he asked, beginning to shut down his laptop. Something in the assistant's pause made Paul abandon his laptop and step straight out of the meeting.

"I'm sorry, Paul, there has been a complication. Your wife's blood pressure is dangerously low. The doctors request that you come immediately."

Paul remembers trying to figure out the quickest route home as he grabbed his things. In the taxi on the way to the station he called Mike and then Mark to ask them to pray. He prayed frantic broken prayers that I would be all right, that the train would go faster than ever before. When he reached Tonbridge he dived from the train and threw himself into a taxi. "Pembury Hospital, please. I need to get there quickly."

The next thing I knew the nurse was telling me not to move.

"You must remain in this position on your side. The uterus is compressing the main aorta." I tried to lift my head and passed out.

"Your husband is here," I heard someone say in the distance. When I finally caught sight of Paul sitting on the seat beside me I couldn't understand why he looked so white and covered in sweat. He did not smile. He clutched my hand without moving. I couldn't speak through the oxygen mask and the drip was partially obscuring my view of him. Two nurses remained at the end of the bed checking my blood pressure every few minutes.

When the consultant entered the room I do not think either he or Paul thought I could hear them. They spoke to each other over the bed.

"What happened?" Paul asked.

"Your wife had a serious vasovagel attack. The poly-hydramnios is causing vena caval compression. This is reducing the return of blood to her heart and brain and causing a dangerous reduction in blood pressure. I have to be honest with you, Mr. Williams, we have something of a dilemma. We need to induce the baby for your wife's safety, but until her blood pressure rises we cannot risk an induction which at thirty-five weeks may not be straightfor-ward and could require either an epidural or an emergency Caesarean. Your wife's blood pressure is too low to permit either. Consequently, we are in a state of limbo. All we can do is wait."

Paul looked exhausted when he sat back down next to me. We still did not speak. I couldn't make the words come out and nor could he.

The Starbucks tea was stone cold when Wren returned to the car seven hours later. She drove back home to fetch Paul an overnight bag. Paul did not want to leave my side. The nursing staff put a mattress on the floor for him.

It was hard to sleep with cramps up one side of my body and the nurse taking my blood pressure every few minutes. I woke from fitful sleep, sweating. I thought about the girls. I remembered how Emilia had pushed me into the ditch to avoid the car and her odd drama the Sunday before. I wondered if she had some instinct that I was in danger. I thought about Paul. How would he have told the children I was dead as well as the baby? It was only by chance that the appointment had been scheduled for that day. What if I had been at home? Would an ambulance have reached me in time? I began to shake as the reality of what had happened hit me. I lay awake for the rest of the night, full of terror. Nothing had prepared me for this.

I couldn't see if Paul was awake, but somehow I sensed it. I pushed the oxygen mask to one side.

"Are you awake?" I whispered.

"Yes."

"What are you thinking?"

"That I nearly lost you."

"It was the one thing we didn't anticipate, wasn't it?"

"Yes. I prayed in the train that you would not die. I was frightened."

"I thought I was dying."

We talked until they brought Paul some breakfast. While he went to wash I thought about the distinction between death and the fear of death. I had come face to face with death the day before, but in the night I had tasted the fear of death. The latter was far more dreadful than the first. We have no control over the timing of death itself, but I could let God come and help me rule the fear of death.

When Paul returned from the bathroom we prayed together. It was awkward praying with the nurse in the room, but our need of prayer was greater than our reserve. We asked God to give us courage to face whatever might happen next. But although we had prayed, fear is insidious. It was not done with us yet.

16

The Garrison

By the time Wren returned to the hospital at ten the next morning I no longer needed the oxygen mask. She helped the nurse give me a sponge bath. I had been in the same clothes for twenty-eight hours. I felt ill and weak. They moved me to the ward later in the day, but when my blood pressure dipped again in the late afternoon, the doctor left swiftly to organize an induction.

"The induction is booked for early tomorrow morning, Mrs. Williams. We will take you down to the labor ward at 7 a.m. to start things off. Clearly we cannot have a repeat of this. We need to get things moving before your blood pressure goes down again and it becomes impossible to intervene should it become necessary during the labor."

I felt very afraid. Paul had gone home with Wren to fetch the children and I was alone. I lay precariously suspended on a tightrope between two fears. On one side there was fear for my own safety and on the other fear for Cerian. What would happen if my blood pressure collapsed again during labor? What would it feel like for Cerian to have her tiny bones crushed as she left the safety of my body? I had to rally all the discipline of mind I could muster just to allay the panic which threatened to overwhelm me on both sides. I held Cerian through the bump. This would be my last night with her.

It was unbearably hot in the ward and my tears became indistinguishable from sweat. Someone had painted the windows shut years ago. I fixed my eyes on the ceiling, not knowing how to pray. Tears poured down my face, filling my ears and soaking the sides of my hair. The curtain moved at my side. I did not look around. I had nothing left. At that moment I wished I had died the day before so I would not have to face the ordeal that awaited me.

The chaplain sat down beside me. "May I pray for you?" I nodded, not moving my eyes from the ceiling.

He took a tiny bottle of oil from his pocket and poured a little onto his finger. Then, gently, he put his finger on my forehead and with the oil he made the sign of the cross. "May the peace of God which transcends all understanding guard your heart and mind in Christ Jesus. May it garrison your mind, like a strong and resilient defense. In the name of the Father, the Son, and the Holy Spirit. Amen."

He slipped away, but the calm he brought did not. The verse of scripture that he quoted was like a rescue harness lifting me from my tightrope to a place of safety. I stretched my arm up in the air as if to grab hold of God. It was easier than praying with words. And in my heart I gave "the Cerian days" back to God and through my tears I thanked him for giving them to me as a gift. I asked him to protect me through the labor and to help Cerian die well.

The thin line between the spiritual and the material dimensions of reality blur at moments of birth, of death, and of intercession. At these moments we are afforded a glimpse of just how thin this line really is. Indeed, we see

perhaps that there is no line at all. We take a second look at
the mundane black-and-white plateau of our existence and
we see that it is, in fact, a textured blaze of color, contoured
with wonder and mystery. And with this glimpse we see that
here good and evil are sharply defined; faith and unbelief are
locked in combat.

Before the chaplain's visit, the fear of death had been
pounding on the door of my mind, terror threatened to seep
right into my heart, and despair had been encircling me.
All were enemies whose one objective was to undermine
my faith. Therefore, I did as an old Sunday school memory
verse requires: I dressed myself in the belt of truth, I put on
the breast plate of righteousness, I covered my head with the
helmet of salvation, I slipped my feet into the shoes of the
gospel of peace, and I took up the shield of faith in one hand
and the sword of the word of God in the other. Then I stood
my ground praying that after I had done everything I would
still be standing. Then I washed my face and brushed my
hair, propped myself up on the pillow, and ate some supper.

Paul made the girls wait while Emma popped in to see me.

"I'm glad to see you!" she said, sitting down beside me.
"Don't do that to me again in a hurry. I think yesterday
ranks as one of the worst nightmares ever." She recounted
the story of having to phone Paul's office while looking out
over the garden at the girls, wondering how they would
react if they discovered I was dead.

"You got more than you bargained for with us, didn't
you, Emma?"

"Just a bit," she grinned. "Don't you worry about the girls.
They're fine." She made her way back out to the corridor to
make space for Hannah and Emilia. The forty-eight hours
I'd been away from them felt like a year. "Cerian will be

born either tomorrow or the next day," I said. "It's time to say goodbye." They both put their heads on the bump and cried their goodbyes, telling their sister they loved her.

I heard Emilia crying in the corridor as she left with Emma. There was nothing I could do to comfort her.

17

Horse and Rider

"How would you two like to sleep in a double bed tonight?" said Marilyn, sticking her head around the curtain.

It was not the first thing we were thinking about, it has to be said. The girls had been gone for an hour, and dazed by a mixture of grief and dread we weren't thinking much beyond the moment.

"I've arranged for you to have the Hope Suite for as long as you need it," Marilyn announced triumphantly.

We had no idea what the Hope Suite was, but "double bed" sounded good and Marilyn's commands were hardly something one would wish to argue with. I was wheeled from the ward just before 9 p.m.

"You will like it in here." Marilyn turned the key in what looked like the door of a flat. She stood back and let us enter. The floors were solid wood, soft curtains hung at the windows, and there were flowers in the hallway. We made our way past a small kitchen and a larger bathroom, to the main room at the end. The staff had drawn the curtains and switched on the four table lights that were positioned tastefully at different points in the spacious room. There was a rug on the floor, a pine chest and bookcase, a rocking chair, and a large, luxurious, terracotta-colored sofa. The bed was pine with a traditional headboard and was laid with what looked like a home-crafted patchwork quilt.

If I say it was like a hotel, that would be right at one level, but the description does not accurately convey the atmosphere of home and tranquility that filled the place. There were no hospital smells or sounds, only the faint cry of seagulls in the distance. The sense of refuge after the horror of the last forty-eight hours was overwhelming. Not only was my mind garrisoned but I felt as if I was physically safe in a walled garden. I lay very still for a long time while Paul unpacked our things.

We found out later that the room had been given to the hospital by a couple and a grandmother who had lost their tiny baby, Hope. They wanted to create a place where people like them could grieve in comfort and peace. We wrote to them afterward expressing our thanks for the beautiful legacy they had left others in the form of a haven in the middle of the ugliness of bereavement. I slept more deeply that night than I had in months.

I woke at five to an unfamiliar sensation in my stomach. Cerian was kicking, not one kick but many. I had rarely felt her move. The excessive quantity of fluid along with the tininess of her body made it almost impossible to feel any movement. I savored the moments with a mixture of joy and agony. She'd woken me up. Did she know that this was her day?

Wren came at 6:30 and made us breakfast. I managed to walk down to the delivery suite, where Marilyn began the induction process.

"You're all remarkably peaceful this morning," she said. "You must have slept well."

Wren, Paul, and I spent the morning reading, listening to music, and talking through the high and low points of Cerian's short life. We also prayed. We prayed for Cerian and for God's mercy on her. We prayed about the birth and we prayed for the staff with whom we would have contact that day. Paul phoned Mark and Janet. It was Becky's birthday.

"We're planning to come to Wren's tonight," Mark said. "Janet's sister is having the girls. We will be there when you want us." We had not dared to think they would come all the way down to Kent, let alone on a family birthday, but the thought of seeing them was like a beacon.

"We're praying you through," Janet remarked as I said goodbye, and I knew it was not just a platitude.

I picked bright yellow flowers in the afternoon while we walked through the hospital gardens in the rain trying to speed up the contractions. They sat on the locker by the bed throughout the delivery like a promise that one day the sun would shine again. I fixed my eyes on them during contractions.

By the middle of the afternoon the contractions began to be sustained and painful. The more painful they became, the more I withdrew. Paul and Wren sat in the lounge adjoining the delivery room which together formed a private area which the staff referred to as the "home away from home." I lay down on the bed with my face to the wall. I felt completely helpless.

"I simply do not know how to do this, Lord," I prayed. "Every contraction is taking Cerian further from me and every inch of my body is resisting labor. I can't do it, I can't do it. Just let me out. I can't go through with this." But I knew there was no way out. I couldn't run away but I couldn't move forward through the experience either. I curled around the bump, immobilized. "God, show me how to cope with this!"

I lay still for a long time.

Then quite suddenly into my mind came the image I had seen during the worship at our church camp. I saw the rider at full gallop on a great black stallion. There was sound, movement, and power in the sight. The hooves were pounding on the earth, sending mud flying in the wake of the creature. The mane streamed and the hair of the rider was full of sweat. I saw the rider as Jesus coming toward me with incredible urgency. I could see it in my mind as clearly as the yellow flowers beside me. He was coming for Cerian. I remembered the words I had written in my journal: *I am coming to deliver you.* The sheer energy of the image stilled my sobbing. The rider was both warrior and lover, frantic for his loved one; coming to rescue her. I knew without doubt there was something in Cerian that ran with similar spirit to meet him. I remembered Emilia's comment when she had heard the heartbeat, "She sounds like a horse running."

"And me Lord?" I whispered. "What do I do?"

I barely needed to ask it as a question. I knew I had to release her to him. It was as though I had to hand her over the walls of a besieged city in the thick of battle so that she could escape unharmed with him. The urgency of the picture galvanized me. And so with every contraction I began to say, "Lord I trust you and I entrust her to you." I began to find grace for each wave of pain and instead of fighting the contractions I began to work with God toward his end in spite of my desire to keep her safely inside my body.

I realized as I went out to find Wren and Paul that this was the mental preparation I needed and through it I could garrison my mind with the courage and peace that the chaplain had prayed for the previous night.

Paul lay down on the floor next to me. "Are you all right?" He fixed me with his eyes so I couldn't escape the question. He knows I'm a tortoise by nature but he wasn't going to let me retreat into my shell. I find solitude much easier than company, even company as close as Paul's. The deeper I feel something, the more aloneness I seek. I looked at his tired face and I knew he wanted to do this with me. Cerian had felt more mine than his because I'd carried her, but he'd carried me. I had to make myself communicate with him.

I told him about the picture of the horse and rider, forcing out the words between contractions. I will never forget what he said to me: "You're only doing what every parent has to do. We have to let Cerian go and give her back to God. One day we will have to let Hannah and Emilia go too. That's the goal of parenthood: releasing them to God. They are his anyway; we are merely guardians. Every contraction may be taking us further from Cerian but they are taking her closer and closer to God where she belongs."

He grabbed his Bible and then for many hours he read me verse after verse between contractions. I meditated on the texts he fed me instead of focusing on the pain. Later Wren took over to give Paul a break; and so between them they carried me. When they ran out of accessible verses Paul read us a Gerard Manley Hopkins poem.

As a dare-gale skylark scanted in a dull cage
  Man's mountain spirit in his bone-house, mean house,
    dwells –
  That bird beyond remembering his free fells;
  This in drudgery, day-labouring-out life's age.

Though aloft on turf or poor low stage,
  Both sing sometímes the sweetest, sweetest spells,
  Yet both droop deadly sómetimes in their cells
Or wring their barriers in bursts of fear or rage.

Not that the sweet-fowl, song-fowl, needs no rest –
Why, hear him, hear him babble and drop down to his nest,
  But his own nest, wild nest, no prison.

Man's spirit will be flesh-bound when found at best,
But uncumberèd: meadow-down is not distressed
  For a rainbow footing it nor he for his bónes rísen.

Soon Cerian would be released like a skylark from her "bone
cage" and one day God would give her a fully restored body
to live in "uncumbered" freedom. Death was not her end but
her beginning, as it will be for me one day.

18

A Rubber Band

The staff changed for the night shift. The new midwife, Stella, was about my age. Cropped unevenly, her jet black hair shot up in irregular tufts under the influence of some powerful hair gel. Her stud earrings extended from her right lobe all the way round the rim of her ear. She wore battered trainers, incongruous against her uniform. It was the atmosphere she brought with her into the room that struck me more forcibly than her appearance. She stood across the room almost defying us to speak to her. When she came toward me her movements were abrupt and harsh.

"How's it going, Sarah?" She left no space for me to answer. "Marilyn's gone home. I'm in charge around here tonight. Anything you need just give me a shout." She left us alone. Wren, Paul, and I looked at one another. I could see Wren's knuckles were white against the arm of the chair. "In charge . . ." she muttered. "I'll show her who's in charge!"

By 11 p.m. the pain in my back was excruciating. The contractions were regular and intense and with each one the agony in my spine reduced me to the edge of blackout. I could not believe it when the doctor announced that I was still only three centimeters dilated.

"We will have to do an epidural," Stella said. There was no point in disagreeing. She was only stating the obvious. She checked my blood pressure again while we waited for the anesthetist. When he arrived he took my wrist and without any verbal preamble he patted the veins on the back of my hand to see where to insert the cannula.

What I feared has come upon me. These words from the book of Job moved across my mind like the message on a screen saver. Wren used to quote this verse at us whenever she discovered that we had been frightfully naughty. I turned my head toward Paul. He was scrutinizing the blood pressure monitor.

"Can I just check that you're aware of her spinal injury?" he asked the anesthetist.

The doctor nodded his reply. "L4, L5, I know," he said. "We're going in here at L2." He showed Paul the spot on my back.

"Is her blood pressure high enough to do an epidural?" Paul came back again.

"It is a little low but it will be fine."

"Are you sure?" I said. I knew we were pushing him but I was suspended on the tightrope of fear once again. Perhaps he felt my fear challenged his professional judgment because he responded swiftly.

"Look," he said, "I've been doing this job for thirty-five years – since you were a baby – so let me get on with it please."

Stella shot the anesthetist an exasperated glance and he shook his head in reply. All I could see from my position were their faces poised over me. I did not trust either of them and inside I was screaming like a terrified animal in a cage. I knew my fear was irrational, but that didn't make it go away. I was still reeling from the shock of my collapse two days earlier.

"I'm sure you know what you're doing," I said, "but . . ."—I couldn't stop myself—"a little compassion would go a long way."

"My wife is nervous of epidurals," Paul interjected, trying to smooth the atmosphere. "Come on," he said to me, "you can do it. You're going to be fine. Soon you will be out of pain. We are not going to let this fear get the better of us. Put your hands on my shoulders and look at me." Neither Stella nor the anesthetist spoke as I sat on the side of the bed and fixed my eyes on Paul's.

The doctor inserted the needle into my spine. "There we are. All over."

As soon as he saw I was all right, Paul darted from the room. I could see him through the open door with his head between his knees.

It was nearly midnight. And then, quite suddenly, just when we needed them, Mike and Liz walked in. Mike steadied Paul with a firm hug and Liz sat with her face level with mine and silently took my hand.

Mike came close to the bed, his voice gentle as it had always been since the day with the pineapple, "I don't know what to say to you, Sarah," he said. "What do you say at a time like this? But I've brought you a gift." He handed me a rubber band. "Where does this band start and where does it end?"

I turned it over in my hand. "It doesn't."

"In the same way God's grace has no beginning and no end; it goes on and on and it will never run out. It's available to you at every moment."

I did not take that rubber band off my wrist for three months, not even to wash.

We agreed to phone Mike's phone when Cerian was born. They left us to find their hotel room for the night. The epidural was beginning to work, and the pain was abating.

19

Flight of the Skylark

I must have fallen sleep. It was one o'clock and Stella stood next to me checking the epidural monitor.

"I don't know why I didn't have one of these things with both the other two," I said as she took my blood pressure. "I can't feel a thing."

"They're great, aren't they? I had one with my son years ago."

"How old is your boy now?" I asked.

"Nearly fifteen. I can't call him a baby anymore. He's at Crowborough Beacon School."

"We used to play hockey against them."

"Yeah, your mom was telling me you grew up around here." She paused. "It's a shame about your baby. You must be feeling pretty bad right now." For the first time she smiled at me. "Your man's had it, I think. I told him to make himself at home. Things are quiet tonight and the delivery room's empty next door. He's crashed out on the bed."

I laughed.

"And your mom's fast asleep on the sofa. She's a nice woman, your mom is. Very kind of . . . gentle." She filled in the blood pressure reading on the chart. "Not many people want their mothers with them these days." She was making her way toward the door when suddenly I wanted her to check Cerian's heartbeat.

"Please may I listen to the baby's heart?" It was the first time I'd asked during the labor. We had requested that there be no monitoring.

"Are you sure you want to?" she said. I nodded.

By now there was far less fluid and I could feel the shape of Cerian's body. There was no gallop this time. The sound was slow and faint.

Cerian was going, and I knew it.

Stella left me. I put my hands tight around Cerian's tiny body.

It was at that moment that the presence of God came powerfully into the room. It was unlike anything I have ever experienced, before or since. Weighty, intimate, holy, the room was full of God. Everything inside me stilled; I hardly dared breathe. His presence was urgent and imme-diate like the rider on the stallion and I knew with certainty that God had come in his love to take a tiny deformed baby home to be with him. There would be no painful bone crushing for Cerian, only the peaceful wonder of God's enfolding presence.

It was later confirmed that she did indeed die at this time. She died just before the final stage of labor of a placental abruption, a painless death caused by the cutting off of the blood supply to her body – something that could happen to any baby. In the end her deformities didn't touch her.

After some moments I called out. Wren came straight in. "What is it?" she said, briskly dispelling the sleep from her face.

"She's gone."

But Wren seemed not to hear me. The moment she
stepped into the room she too was stilled as I had been.
"God is here," she whispered, kneeling down beside me.
"God is here."

We sat still for a long time. I wanted to call Paul but
neither of us moved. It was not a time for noise or words.

Things happened quite quickly then. Wren went to wake
Paul. Stella fetched the doctor. I started to vomit and the
pain became more intense. The final stage was upon us. It
was the worst of all. I tried to push but my body would not
respond. I had no will to push – who wants to give birth not
to life, but to death? There was nothing left to look forward
to. I felt abandoned and desolate. God had come and taken
Cerian home but he had left me behind. It was the worst
hour of my life.

Paul didn't know Cerian was already dead. I knew instinc-
tively that I could not go through the last stage without his
courage and hope.

Finally she came, with a huge explosion of blood that
hit the wall and covered the doctor's face and gown. Wren
clapped a hand over her mouth to stifle a scream. The abruption had caused hemorrhaging behind the placenta. But I
was barely aware of the staff flustering over my loss of blood,
removing the clot, and stitching me back up. All I knew was
they had taken Cerian away. I thought I heard her cry, but I
knew she was dead. Paul was with Cerian. The pediatrician
was talking to him. I shouted, "Is she alive?" but I knew she
was dead. I could hear wailing. It was some time before I
realized the strange, anguished howling was me.

I still thought she might be alive when Paul brought her
to me wrapped in the soft, white fleece we'd so carefully
prepared. There was blood on the fleece. Paul's face told me

she was dead but still I hoped even though I knew. I turned my head away. I couldn't hold her yet. I shook. Paul passed the baby to Wren and he held me. I wanted to cry but I could only wail.

20

A Whole Lifetime Over

Eventually, they put Cerian in my arms. I was repulsed and
yet compelled by her tiny form. She was still warm from my
body but she was dark purple and her color shocked me. I
had been warned, but still I was shocked. She had been dead
for three hours. I kissed her forehead.

There were lots of things I wanted to say to her; things I
wanted to pray but no words came out. I could not sustain
a thought from one end to the other. When Mike came
he took Cerian in his arms and he prayed all that I wanted
to say. He gently put structure around what we could not
articulate.

Wren washed Cerian in a baby bath at the end of the
bed. "Please let me do this. It's about all I can do for her as
a grandma." She quietly extracted the poised flannel from
Stella's hand.

It was the first time I'd seen Cerian's deformity. I did
not want to look at her at first. Her body frightened me.
But Wren's loving attention gave her dignity in a way that
I could not bring myself to do alone. Slowly I was able to
follow Wren's lead.

It was strange that she was so very deformed because all my thoughts of her had been filled with beauty and there was a shattering disjunction between the physical body that lay in front of me and the relationship that I had had with her spirit. I do not want to describe Cerian's body. I will keep this in my heart. But the comfort I gained from looking at her was this: she had a body, which was suited for the purpose God had for her. It was not a body that could ever have walked or run or cuddled, but for the purpose of being inside me, her body was perfect.

Wren dressed Cerian in a tiny embroidered cream silk dress that Paul had bought for her. She put the bonnet from Emma on Cerian's head and she wrapped her in the shawl. Finally, she put the booties Hannah had made on Cerian's tiny feet.

Stella cut a lock of her hair and made a print of both her hand and her foot. We took as many photographs as we could. It was not a natural thing to take photographs; it jarred. But now I am grateful for them. Wren laid Cerian in a Moses basket and covered her with the quilt embroidered with her initials. She looked beautiful. I ached.

Paul took Cerian and set her beside him in the adjoining lounge while the staff washed and redressed me. I was still vomiting even after they had sponged me down.

"That just about sums up the pregnancy, doesn't it?" I said, passing a last bowlful of vomit to Wren.

"I am proud of you," she said.

It was only later that I discovered this was Paul's darkest hour. He sat in the gloom of the lounge with Cerian's body next to him. He had no energy left to support me anymore. His own pain and loss were acute. Now Cerian had come, he realized the full force of what he'd lost. He held onto

the image he had seen of her in his dream. It was the only
time he had touched her alive accept for the tiny fluttering
through the wall of my stomach and the mass of grey and
white on the computer screen. But he loved her a whole
lifetime over.

Paul called Mark shortly after Cerian was born and it
was not long before he arrived at the labor ward. I did not
see him. He'd come for Paul. When Mark walked through
the door of the "home away from home" suite Paul left his
dark chair in the corner and sobbed. In the privacy of their
friendship there was no one Paul had to be strong for and
he was able to let out the raw mixture of emotions that I
couldn't have handled at that time. Mark was unperturbed
as Paul moved from grief to anger to guilt and then back
to grief again. He understood the strange way in which
manhood, even prowess, is linked almost primevally to the
ability to produce healthy offspring. So many men are never
able to voice this unconscious link and it can eat away at
them over many years. Mark helped Paul bring the myriad
of conflicting reactions into the open.

Mark left just before the staff took us back to the Hope
Suite. He went back to Wren's house where he and Janet
spent most of the day playing with the girls and giving
Emma a much-needed break.

Just before we left the labor suite, the anesthetist put his
head around the door. "I'm about to turn in." Bashfully,
he added, "I'm sorry about your baby, and, er, I came to
say . . . what you said to me last night about compassion was
absolutely right and I want to apologize."

I smiled at him. "Thank you for coming to speak to me."

Stella was also going off duty. She lingered in the room
clearing up various bits on the counter behind the bed. She

seized a moment when no one else was in the room and came straight over to stand next to me. "It's very sad what happened."

"Yes it is. Thanks for looking after me," I tried to make it easy for her to leave. Her face contorted into what looked at first like an ugly grimace, until I realized she was dissolving into tears.

"You're a brave lady." She fled the room sobbing.

I don't know what became of Stella but I do know she was not in charge that night.

21

The Seagulls' Cry

They took me back to the Hope Suite on a hospital bed. I'd
been in labor for twenty-two hours. Paul placed Cerian's
Moses basket next to the pine bed and I sank into troubled
sleep. When I woke to the sight of Cerian's purple face, panic
gripped me. Grabbing my stomach, I screamed. Paul tried to
hold my hand.

"Are the girls all right? Paul, I have to know if the girls are
all right! I have to go to the girls. They may be hurt." The
trauma crashed over me. I tried to climb off the bed but my
legs gave way when I caught sight of Cerian again. I thought
she was breathing. I hadn't fed her. Had I killed her? Her
body frightened me – my body frightened me.

Paul took my hands and began to pray quietly. Paul took
his battered Bible and above my broken cries he read:

Though you have made me see troubles,
   many and bitter,
   you will restore my life again;
from the depths of the earth
   you will again bring me up.
You will increase my honor
and comfort me once more.
(Psalm 71:20–21)

When he reached the end, he read the words again twice. In the distance I could hear the faint sound of the seagulls. All would be well, but I realized it would be a long, slow climb through the grief and I needed to be very gentle with myself. I was terribly vulnerable. In my Bible I have etched the date in the margin by the psalm Paul read me on that day: Saturday, August 31, Cerian's birthday.

I didn't panic like that again. As I look back on it, I realize how very normal such panic was after the trauma and the shock. Once Cerian died the protective shell in which we were encased in order to survive through the pregnancy was stripped away and we felt the grief.

When I'd settled, Paul went to collect the children. I will never know what their faces looked like when Paul told them their sister was dead. Janet told me later she heard them cry from the next room. She walked out into the garden at the sound, holding her own bump and trying to ward off fear for her own little one.

When the children arrived at the hospital Emilia strode straight across the room to Wren, who was holding the baby. She held out her bunch of flowers as if she expected Cerian to take them. Wren took the flowers and showed Emilia the baby. Like Wren, Emilia's first instinct was to hold Cerian. Only the expression on her face showed that she knew this was not a living child. "Why is she so purple, Wren? She looks like a plum. Why is Cerian cold?"

White-faced, Hannah lingered on the threshold with Emma until finally she threw herself onto the bed next to me. "That's not Cerian!" she cried. "That's not her!" I took the crumpled card from Hannah's hand and tried to smooth it out. *I love you little sister,* it said. All I wanted to say was, "I'm so sorry I couldn't give you another sister." Hannah's distress was acute. I held her close to me for a long time and then abruptly she needed to talk. She wanted to know everything about the birth, when Cerian had died, and how I felt. She would not look at the body. She seemed to relax when I told her that I had not really wanted to hold Cerian at first.

The nurse stuck her head around the door. "Are you all right? Have you got everything you need? I am sorry about the noise!"

"Thanks, we're fine," I told her. To Paul I added, "I can't hear any noise."

Meanwhile, Wren was having her work cut out to prize Emilia away from Cerian. "Why is her nose all funny, Wren? Why are her eyes closed like that? Has she got any arms?" Except for her face, Cerian was completely covered when the girls saw her. Seeing her face was enough. They did not need to take on board the detail of the rest of her body. We were glad that we'd done it like this.

Emma stood in the doorway looking awkward. I called her over to sit with Hannah and me on the bed.

"You look more exhausted than I do," I said to her.

But Emma was completely focused on Hannah. "I'm not sure I could do what Emilia's doing right now, could you, Han? Has she got your booties on, Han?" For the first time Hannah looked over at the body. Wren put the baby in the basket and took Emilia out to the kitchen. Emma took Hannah's hand and together they went over to look at Cerian. They both stood at a distance and peered.

"I can't see," said Hannah. Emma took her closer and bent over the basket. Pulling back the shawl slightly, they both looked in. The booties were there. Emma gave Hannah a hug and they sat down on the sofa next to each other.

"Do you want to hold her?" Emma asked.

"Not sure," said Hannah, "Kind of yes, kind of no."

"Same here," said Emma. For half an hour they sat there talking. Every so often Hannah returned to the question, "Shall I hold her? I'm not sure." Emma was careful not to push her.

"I will hold her after you," Emma said finally.

Paul passed Cerian to Hannah. Hannah held her and her tears fell on the white, spidery shawl.

"I did it, Emma," she said triumphantly.

Emma held Cerian too and I thought about the bonnet she had given her.

After the girls said goodbye, Mark and Janet came in briefly. Janet told me all about Wren's garden, the girls, the dogs, and the woods while Mark held Cerian, as he has all our children. None of us expected Janet to hold her. But as Mark put Cerian back into the basket Janet asked bravely if she could hold Cerian. It was hard to see the incongruity of her tummy brimful of life, pressed against Cerian's cold body. "She's like a little china doll," Janet said.

Holding Cerian felt like the ultimate expression of love, to us. It is not easy to hold a dead baby and their acceptance of Cerian was a recognition of the depth of our feeling for her, and an acknowledgement of her personhood.

"The drink can wait a bit, mate." Mark said to Paul as they left. "But don't think you are getting out of it that lightly. You're buying this time."

Paul and I were alone, and we knew that the moment we'd been dreading had come. We had to say goodbye.

We said nothing to each other. What could we say? Paul took Cerian in his arms. He held her away from his body and looked at her for a long time. Eventually he passed her to me. I touched her cold cheek. The nurse came to take the body away.

Seeing the basket containing her disappear through the doorway was worse than physical pain. When the door closed on our daughter there was nothing but the void where she should have been. Although I had anticipated her going so many times, until this moment I had been full of her. It was the first real taste of loss. Even though I knew she was with God, it didn't insulate me from the pain.

I crawled to the bed, curled up small, and cried.

Paul said nothing. Quietly, almost imperceptibly, he cleared up the room, straightened the sofa, turned on the small lamps, and drew the curtains. He took the table on which the Moses basket had been a moment ago, pulled it away from the wall, and placed one yellow candle in the middle. Around the candle he arranged the flowers from Emilia, Hannah's crumpled card, and the bright yellow dress. When the nurse came back with Cerian's clothes, he placed the booties, the bonnet, and the quilt on the table. He draped the shawl across the back along with his own silk gift and the tiny hospital wristband. His silent actions comforted me far more than words could have done. The table seemed to say: *She has gone, but not the memories.*

"I'm sorry about the noise," the nurse said again as she came in with a cup of tea the next morning. "It's the only problem with this room." Paul and I looked at each other, bemused. "Paul, the doctor is expecting you at 10 o'clock and the registrar of deaths should be free at 11."

While I wrote in my journal Paul handled the paperwork. He returned an hour and a half later looking exhausted and clutching a stark certificate on which the word "Stillbirth" stood out in bold letters.

We got ready to leave. On our way out the head nurse came to say goodbye. "I do hope the noise has not disturbed you too badly."

I had to find out what they were talking about. "Do you mean the seagulls?" I asked.

"Seagulls?" It was her turn to look bemused. "I don't think there are any seagulls here."

Strangely, the fact that we were fifty miles inland had not occurred to me until then.

The nurse said, "It's the sound of babies crying on Ward 4."

I looked down at the rubber band on my wrist. "Thank you, God," I whispered. "I could not have coped with babies crying. Please let me carry on hearing seagulls for a while."

22

No Morning in Heaven

After Cerian's death the word "paradox" took on poignant meaning for me. Throughout her life I had experienced entirely different and apparently contradictory things at once: grief and hope, pain and joy, ugliness and beauty, weakness and strength. This experience of paradox did not end with her death but it deepened still further in the time of mourning that followed. The funeral itself embodied this paradox. I encountered it again as I returned to work and, most of all, I faced it in a stark way as I began to consider anew the culture of which I am a part.

"I keep calling it Cerian's wedding," I remarked to Paul after I had mixed up funeral and wedding for the fifth time. "My brain is scrambled."

"Maybe it is not such a bad description. It is a celebration after all," he said. As I existed in a vacuum of loss in the days immediately after Cerian's death, Paul worked with energy and focus to organize the funeral. He had a clear vision of what he wanted the day to be like, and his determination carried the rest of us. He gathered the music that had been special to us during the pregnancy, he asked Mark to lead the worship at the thanksgiving, and Mike to conduct the service and the ceremony at the crematorium. Our neighbor Adrienne, whose baby I'd held on that first day in May, agreed to arrange the flowers for us. Paul selected Bible readings which had been our anchor points for the last nine months and he invited all the people who had carried us through. He had Hopkins's skylark poem printed on the order of service. He ordered lavish quantities of bright yellow flowers and he planned a supper party for our family and closest friends at our friend Sissel's house after the crematorium. He even had Cerian's name engraved on a tiny brass plaque and fixed to the top of her coffin. Every detail expressed the beauty of her life and our pride in her. It was only other people who saw incongruity in the paradox of loss and celebration.

"Why have a banquet for a stillborn child anyway?" The florist didn't actually say this but we all sensed she would have liked to as she snapped impatiently at us deliberating over the flowers. At the department store the checkout lady asked me if the large quantity of bright yellow ribbons, candles, and napkins were for a special occasion. She looked bemused when I said, "Yes. They're for my daughter's funeral." After this exchange I struggled to find my way back to the car through my tears. I had to pray I would hear the sound of the seagulls in my head again.

I touched the same paradox the day before the funeral. Over and over I thought: *Tomorrow I bury my daughter. Tomorrow I bury my daughter.* I wandered around the house aimlessly. My arms were the biggest problem. They should have been holding something, but instead they hung like clumsy, redundant objects at my side. I kept folding them across my chest, and stuffing my hands inside my sleeves. In the end I resorted to hugging a hot water bottle and rocking myself on the sofa. No one had told me how physical it is to lose a baby.

"I can't do this," I murmured. In the night I woke three times, thinking surely it must be time to feed her now. When I finally got up on the morning of the 13th September I found a card on my dressing table with a tiny bunch of flowers. Wren had had a restless night too and in her handwriting I read the words from 2 Corinthians 12:

> "My grace is sufficient for you, for my power is made perfect in weakness." Therefore I will boast all the more gladly about my weaknesses, so that Christ's power may rest on me. . . . For when I am weak, then I am strong.

I had nothing to bring to the day except my weakness.

The service went as planned, but I had little sense of it. I was aware of faces all around me. There was sound and movement but it all seemed a long way off. I felt suspended alone with Cerian in some other place and I wished there were two coffins at the front of the church. I imagined a larger one for me nestling close to the miniature version that looked so forlorn, set at a distance from the congregation.

When I stood up to pay my tribute to Cerian I had no idea if words would come out of my mouth. I was dazed by the array of grave faces turned toward me. I looked at them for some time wondering if they had any idea what abject pain I was feeling in my heart at that moment. They were close to me in terms of proximity and some of them close to me through ties of family and deep friendship; but just then I felt as though I was looking at them all, even Paul, Hannah, and Emilia, from another shore. I'd known Cerian intimately; I'd enveloped her in my own body and protected her as part of myself.

At that moment I felt closer to her than I did to any of them and I wanted to be with her. I turned to one side to let my eyes rest on her coffin and addressed her one last time:

People normally write tributes to recollect the memorable things that loved ones have done and to celebrate their achievements. You do not have any achievements for us to celebrate, Cerian. You spent your short life resting in a hidden place.

But had you lived a long life crammed full of accomplishment, I could not have been more grateful to God for you, nor could your life have had more value and significance for me. I am so grateful to you for taking me to a quiet place of intimacy with God – for giving me a glimpse of the nature of his love.

There was nothing you had to do to earn my love. I didn't require anything from you before I loved you. I loved you simply because you were mine.

Your worth was written into your being from the very first moment of your existence. The value of your person was not measured by your usefulness, nor was your identity composed of hard-won achievements, or the gleanings of experience.

Thank you for helping me hear an echo of God's eternal love. Thank you for giving me a message and a song. You whispered a message to me in the secret place but I will shout it out. I will shout to a world afflicted by anxiety, obsessed with strength, afraid of weakness, outraged by deformity, and intimidated by death.

You were precious, Cerian, because you were created and given as a gift. I am privileged to have carried you and I honor you and all that your life has been.

No one moved. I sat back down in the silence.

It was some time before Paul's voice filled the auditorium. "Cerian is Welsh for 'loved one.' The word is a general term of endearment like 'my darling.' If God were Welsh he would call each of us 'Cerian–my loved one.' Cerian's life message was to demonstrate this love and she has spoken her message well."

Paul sat back down next to me and took my hand.

The service ended with the hymn "The King of Love My Shepherd Is." The congregation dispersed to the reception we had planned for them. The undertaker let us take the tiny coffin in our own car to the crematorium so that Cerian could be with us for one last journey. As we pulled in to park by the "Chapel of Rest," Emilia said, "Why did Mike say there would be no mourning in heaven?" Out of the corner of my eye I could see Paul preparing an intense theological answer. But Emilia carried on. "If there is no morning in heaven, when will Cerian wake up?"

Despite the extremity of the moment, we all began to laugh. The sun was shining and the sorrow was tinged with an odd sense of festivity. We were surrounded by those we loved most. My oldest school friend was there; others had traveled down from Birmingham and Northumberland and up from Kent. Mark and Janet had brought the children with them.

Later, when the curtain finally obscured Cerian's coffin from view, Emilia raised her hand and waved goodbye. The tears streamed down her face onto her bright pink dress and Hannah whispered, "Adieu."

Paul and I had no other language but tears and they came like waves. We clung to one another but there was relief in tears after many days of numbness. I let the distance flood between me and Cerian and I began to connect with others again.

I remember almost nothing about the rest of the day except the light, the golden flowers, and the sense of love, family, and belonging. It was a fitting end. The day – like Cerian's whole life – was filled with a mixture of pain and beauty, bereavement and joy.

23

Married and Male

I spent the autumn season grieving intensely for Cerian, but it was clean grief in which I felt no guilt or regret. People said the journey of grief would take me through many different stages—shock, denial, anger, even depression. But I didn't seem to journey very far. All I did was revolve around one small thing: I missed her, whichever way I looked at it. The loss came in unexpected waves—when I found a pair of white baby tights stuffed at the back of Emilia's sock drawer, or when I found myself in the diaper aisle at the supermarket. I poured my energy into making a large album of photographs, poems, quotes, Bible verses, pictures the children had drawn, and flowers I had collected, to preserve the memories of the pregnancy. I found a small mid-nineteenth-century elm chest in an antique shop in the village of Burford, just outside Oxford. I used it to keep safe the precious things we made for Cerian.

It was not until late autumn that the letter notifying us of the appointment to review the postmortem arrived. It was addressed to *Ms. Williams.*

"There's no mention of me," said Paul as we sat at the breakfast table. "They haven't even included my name in the letter. It is not as if they think you are unmarried."

I suddenly remembered a poor joke I had read in a glossy magazine while waiting to have my hair cut: "Motherhood is a fact, paternity merely a hypothesis." For the first time I understood what was meant by the anger stage of grief. I was angry – blindingly angry. Paul had arranged the postmortem, he had chivvied the doctors along, he had watched over the proceedings, taking care to ensure that the restrictions we had placed on the postmortem were respected, and they hadn't even had the courtesy to include his name in the letter.

I got up from the table and grabbed the phone. "Can you put me through to the secretary of the prenatal diagnosis unit please." There was a pause.

Paul looked at me bemused. "What are you doing?" he hissed.

I turned away from him so I wouldn't lose my nerve.

"Prenatal diagnosis, can I help you?"

"Yes, hello. Am I speaking to . . . ?" I read the name on the bottom of the letter, "secretary of the prenatal diagnosis unit?"

"Yes, how can I help?"

"I have just received a letter from you informing me of the date and time of a meeting with the consultant to discuss the results of our daughter's postmortem examination."

"Oh yes, Ms. Williams is it? What can I do to help?"

"I know this may seem a rather a strange question, but would you mind telling me why you wrote *Ms. Williams* at the top of the letter?" There was a pause at the other end of the line. "You see," I continued, "I am married and my husband's name is Paul."

"Yes, Ms. Williams, I know that."

I paused this time. "Then why didn't you address the letter to Mr. and Mrs. Williams?"

"Oh, it's standard practice for us to write just to the mother."

"Can you explain why that should be so?" I pressed.

"It's hospital policy."

"I understand that, but can you explain why?" My voice was unduly calm but inside I was raging.

"It is not my decision, Ms. Williams. We are told to do it this way."

"I do appreciate that, but I would be very grateful if you could explain why?"

"It is considered best etiquette. We don't wish to offend unmarried mothers."

"I see. What about the offense caused to married women, to fathers, and to married fathers?" I said. It was difficult to keep my voice under control. "I do understand that this is not your decision individually, but can you please rewrite your letter to us. You see – I am offended. I'm not Ms. Williams, I am *Mrs.* Williams, and I am offended that I should be addressed in any other way in this context. My husband is also offended. It is as much his daughter that we are coming to the hospital to discuss. And can you please formally relay the fact that this hospital policy of exclusion is deeply offensive to us."

Paul squirmed in his chair. "Steady on," I heard him say.

"I didn't raise my voice, did I?" I said in defense as I replaced the handset, shaking slightly.

"Well, no . . . but I think she got the message loud and clear all the same. Poor woman. It's not her fault."

"Then whose fault is it? The system doesn't have a name or a face, otherwise I'd find out who it is and give it to them straight. That would be easier. Someone's got to say something. In the space of one generation it has become politically incorrect to be married and male."

"Making her rewrite the letter may have been a little steep."

"But language is important – really important. You can say it's only a form of words, but language bullies us into conforming to a social standard that I don't want to be part of."

"You get called Ms. every day in bank and business letters. Why are you so angry about it now all of sudden?"

"It's the spirit of that place I can't stand. I don't really know what it is, but it feels all wrong to me and the Ms. is just one symptom of it. It's hard to put it into words."

"Well try," said Paul, "because you are beginning to sound like a reactionary."

"Look at this." I grabbed a copy of the *Times* and began to read: "'Yet while a fetus is being saved in one operating theater, a termination for "social reasons" may well be taking place in the next theater on a fetus at exactly the same stage of development.'* Somehow in my mind that unit seems to sit right between these two operating theaters mediating the whole business of human quality control." I remembered how we had sat in the car looking out across at the two entrances to the Women's Center just after our third scan with Cerian.

"But you can't blame the prenatal diagnosis unit for that. They're only doing what individual people want them to do."

"Demand and supply – that's such an economist's answer." Now we were teetering on the brink of a fight.

* Sunday Times of London, July 4, 2004

"It's true!" he said. "It is the demands of individuals that justify the resource allocation and drive all the spin-off technologies." Paul lowered his voice and we both looked across the kitchen table to the spot where the highchair should have been.

"Paul, would you adopt a severely mentally and physically handicapped child?"

He looked at me and after some time he said: "Would I adopt Cerian, is that what you mean?"

And I knew from the look of love and sadness in his eyes that the answer was yes, a hundred times over, yes. Demand and supply is all very well but it is premised on choice. We didn't choose Cerian and now we didn't have the option to choose her again. She was a gift. Maybe we can control demand and supply but we can't control a gift.

I cleared the table, shoved the washing into the machine, and stomped around the house feeling ineffectual against the great giant of culture.

Two days later a letter arrived addressed to Mr. and Mrs. Williams. It was hardly a slaying of Goliath, but I smiled when I opened it and I replied immediately, thanking the secretary for the letter and for her help in organizing the postmortem.

My confidence rapidly dissolved, however, when a week later we walked through the entrance to the prenatal diagnosis unit to attend the actual meeting.

"I think I am going to faint," I said, leaning heavily on Paul's arm. "I can't go back in there."

Paul led me forward to the reception desk, where I hid behind him.

"We've come to see the consultant. Mr. and Mrs. Williams."

"Your name, please."

"Williams," said Paul.

"No, *your* name, please?" The receptionist bypassed Paul with her gaze and spoke directly to me. "Your name, please." Paul was holding me up.

"I need to know *your* name, please." The receptionist was staring at me resolutely.

"Mrs. Williams," I said finally. At which point she signed the form, picked up the phone, and notified the consultant of our arrival.

"Unbelievable," said Paul as we sat down in the waiting room.

"You see? It isn't just my imagination, is it?"

"I never said it was. She didn't even look at me!"

"Maybe that's hospital policy too," I whispered.

The meeting was both civil and reassuring, despite the reception.

"Well, it has been good to meet you, Mr. and Mrs. Williams." The consultant rose to shake our hands after having spent half an hour explaining the medical details to us. "It is reassuring to know that there is no reason at all why this condition should recur. Technically, you have a slightly higher statistical chance of recurrence than you would have done if this had never happened at all, but there is still roughly only a one in seven hundred thousand probability of recurrence. I hope we shall be seeing you here again very soon under better circumstances."

"The trouble is," I said as we made our way back to the car, "you can never replace a person."

24

The Shaming of the Strong

I touched the paradox again when I returned to work at the university just after Christmas. Going back to work was the bleakest part of the grieving process. I opened the door of my study and looked at my bookshelves. I felt old, tired, and empty. I revisited the toilet where I had first been sick. I was back in the same place, at the same time of year, with nothing to show for it except my fatigue. Everyone moved so fast and talked so loud. Life crashed back like a tide and I was raw and vulnerable.

"How are you?" beamed a visiting professor at lunch during my first week back. "Last time I saw you . . ." She pointed at my tummy with a conspiratorial smile. "So how's your baby? It must be about four months old by now. Did you have a boy or a girl?"

The yogurt I'd been eating glazed over in front of me. "Dead," I said. It was the only word I could get out of my mouth. I didn't wait to observe her response. I simply fled.

A week later the same thing happened again. A new lecturer introduced himself as I sat down to consume a rapid lunch between tutorials. "I haven't met you yet. I'm new here." He shook my hand. "I came in October. I think you were away last term?"

"Yes," I said. "I was on leave."

"Somewhere nice?" He dug into the casserole.

"No." Perhaps he should have heard the note of warning in my voice, but perhaps I was asking too much.

"Oh, come on, you must have done something fun? Interesting research project?"

I said, "I was on maternity leave." And before he could interject with yet another comment I added, "My daughter died." I don't remember ever seeing that lecturer again. His skill in avoiding me was unrivaled.

But he was not the only one who avoided me. When I approached, people suddenly seemed to forget things and scuttle back into their offices. On one occasion I even saw the tip of a colleague's skirt disappear into the broom closet when I turned into the main corridor. Those who couldn't escape me avoided direct eye contact and steered conversations onto safe, busy ground. I felt the isolation of ongoing grief. Even Paul seemed to have settled back into a rhythm of life and work, and I found it increasingly difficult to share the persistent sense of loss with him or with anyone else. Mike and Liz had warned me that grief is both a long and lonely journey, but still the experience caught me off balance.

I remained in this state of internal distance until one memorable day in early May. I had organized a lecture in college by a Catholic theologian named Heather Ward. Knowing that her topic, the gift of self, would be both contentious and explicitly Christian, I only invited those I thought would be sympathetic. As I left the building on the day of the event to dash home and put the children to bed before the evening lecture began, I met my feminist colleague. I had been avoiding her. The memory of our difficult conversation the previous May had not left me yet.

I lingered in the college lodge checking and re-checking my mail. But she lingered too.

Eventually, she asked me the inevitable question: "How are you, Sarah?"

I hesitated and continued to fumble with my mail. "Oh, okay, thanks. Teaching is as busy as ever. I've got a heavy load this term, but I'm surviving." *That was pathetic, Sarah,* I said to myself. *For goodness' sake, be real.* "Actually, life is quite hard just now. I'm still grieving, to be honest, and it is hard to be back at work."

"I'm so sorry. It must be very hard."

It was a simple, heartfelt response and it connected us.

"Have you got time for a drink before you head home?" she asked.

"I'm afraid not. I've got to tuck the children in and get back here for a 7:30 lecture." I bit my tongue – too late.

"A lecture? Here in college? I didn't know about that. What's it on?"

"The gift of self."

"That sounds interesting. Who's it by?"

"Dr. Heather Ward."

"Who is she?"

There was no way back now. I would have to explain. "A Catholic theologian who's interested in how different historical periods have understood ideas of personhood."

"Sounds really interesting. Why didn't you tell me it was on?"

"I must go," I called over my shoulder as I headed for the parking lot.

I was late getting back to the college. Emilia had had what she called "a highly horrible day" and I sat on the end of her bed until she fell asleep. By the time I got to the lecture

room the only vacant seats were at the back. I was relieved
I'd asked a graduate student to introduce the speaker, and I
tried not to sound out of breath as I slipped into the back row
and hid behind my officious pad of paper.

"What is the self?" Heather began. "What is it that
constitutes human personhood? Our culture regards individual agency as the key to selfhood. We spend our time
removing the blockages to our emotional and imaginative
life and therefore to our social relations. We shape our
personalities and we build our characters. We derive our
sense of worth and meaning from our abilities, talents, and
achievements and most of all from our capacity to make
decisions for ourselves."

My note-taking ceased and in my head I shouted: *What
happens if you can't choose, if you can't make decisions for yourself, if you're stripped of agency unexpectedly, through illness or
disability? Does this make you a sub-person or a non-person? Are
you a pre-person before you achieve anything? And if you are born
with no talents and you cannot achieve the proper formation of the
body in the womb, does this mean you are not a person?*

We were ten minutes into the talk when my feminist
colleague walked in. The only seat left was next to me. She
slid into the row and sat down. I smiled politely and prayed,
Oh God, I'm so scared of her!

"But Christian theology stands at odds with these cultural
definitions of personhood. It is relationality that lies at the
heart of Christian definitions of personhood. All Christian
thinking on the subject of personhood begins with the truth
that human beings are made in the image of a Trinitarian
God who is by nature love. God the Father, God the Son,
God the Holy Spirit exist in a dynamic inter-relationship
that *is* love. God does not simply act lovingly; he is in his

very person love. To bear the image of God is to be loved by
a relational God who in love created us as relational beings.
Even though the image of God is marred in all of us as a
result of sin, our intrinsic worth as human creatures resides
not in our qualities, characters, or achievements, nor in
our physical bodies or mental capacities, but in the eternal
character of God. We treat one another with dignity because
of the intrinsic worth of every person as a relational being
loved by God."

I sat back in my chair and allowed the words to sink
deep into me. I had absolutely no doubt that Cerian was
loved intimately and personally by God. This way of
understanding the human person resonated so deeply with
my experience in carrying Cerian that I felt as if I had come
home. I wanted to hold the words tight, and to be held
by them. Cerian's worth was related to her being, not her
functional utility. And in the same way this God who is love
created me. My intrinsic worth as a human being is prior
to and irrespective of anything else about me. I am loved
in exactly the same way that Cerian is loved. I looked up at
the portraits of worthy masters, great scholars, and leaders
that covered the walls of the room. All the privilege of my
education, my skills as a teacher and a thinker, being here at
Oxford, the talents and attributes I possess, my healthy body,
my husband, my children – all the things out of which I had
composed my identity, my sense of self, and my sense of
worth – were good gifts but they do not define who I am, nor
do they define my worth. Cerian had none of these things,
but the absence of them makes her no less a person than me.

Heather concluded: "If selfhood is found in our relationship with God, then it follows that our responsiveness
to him, our receptivity to his spirit, our giving of love to

others, and our receiving of love from them define the quality of our lives. Being fully human involves a reorientation of our wills and our desires toward God himself. He is at the center of our existence, not us. At times this reorientation of the person toward God may feel like a loss of self, when it is in fact quite the opposite. We receive our identity from him as a gift."

I looked back on the months I'd spent with Cerian. When I first found out about her deformity and made the choice to carry her to term, it felt like the destruction of my plans and hopes. It went against what I wanted. It limited me. But it was in this place of limitation that God showed me more of his love. Up until this point, the clamor of my desires and wishes had made me a closed system centered on myself, on my needs, flaws, and attributes. My life, even at times my religion, had revolved around achievement, reputation, and winning respect and approval from others. I had busied myself with perfect home, perfect children, perfect job, all the things I wanted. I had become joyless, controlled, and predictable. I had no passion and even less compassion; I was too busy to care. I knew I had lost something deep and precious, but I didn't know what it was. And the more I felt the lack of it, the harder I tried to find it through effort.

During the nine months I carried Cerian, God had come close to me again unexpectedly, wild and beautiful, good and gracious. I touched his presence as I carried Cerian, and as a result I realized that underneath all my other longings lay an aching desire for God himself and for his love. Cerian shamed my strength and in her weakness and vulnerability she showed me a way of intimacy. The verses in 1 Corinthians 1:27–29 came alive to me in a completely different way.

But God chose the foolish things of the world to shame the wise; God chose the weak things of the world to shame the strong. God chose the lowly things of this world and the despised things – and the things that are not – to nullify the things that are, so that no one may boast before him.

Cerian was weak by one set of criteria and by the same criteria I was strong, but the beauty and completeness of her personhood nullified the value system to which I had subscribed for so long.

There was silence when Heather finished and then with quiet dignity she answered question after question as hands flew up all over the room. An hour later she ended the session and a long queue developed for further informal questioning.

My colleague didn't move. She sat with her eyes fixed straight ahead.

"I used to believe in God," she said eventually. "I wish I still could."

There was something in the way she said it that moved me. I put my hand on her arm and we sat there in silence. In the absence of words I imagined myself taking her by the hand and bringing her into the presence of God, into the love we had just heard about. I felt a nudge in my heart and with trepidation I turned to look her straight in the eyes. "God does not rape, you know."

After a moment when I wondered if she would ever speak to me again, tears slowly welled up in her eyes and she whispered, "But people do."

It was a tiny key that unlocked her heart. Few weeks pass now when we do not talk to each other. We talk of many things but mainly life, pain, and faith. We have become close friends.

I realize looking back that I was in danger at that time of getting locked in my own sorrow and grief and cutting myself off from other people. My colleague showed me something important, and her friendship drew me out of myself. Everyone hurts. At some stage all of us find that life does not deliver what we expected. Sometimes other people hurt us directly. We all hit the boundaries of our capacity at some time or other. Often we have little power to prevent difficult and painful things. Although we can use our strength to protect ourselves, our autonomy to isolate ourselves, and all the resources of our will and agency to try to control outcomes, the freedom we create for ourselves is illusory and terribly fragile. Ultimately, this fragile freedom of autonomy depends on us and it is, therefore, as limited as we are. But true human freedom comes from the limitless love of God, in which "we live and move and have our being." God lavished his love on us in the person of Jesus Christ. It was his choice to lay aside his freedom and to limit himself for us which enables us to enjoy God's love forever. Nothing–not even death can limit this love. Our choices may be limited but our freedom is not.

25

The Bird Tree

The girls too were changed. Emilia, despite her ongoing struggle with chronic illness, developed an antenna for other people's pain. At the end of the church service each Sunday she would disappear to give someone a hug or simply to say hello to outsiders. She even went up to a little boy on the bus one day. The boy was crying uncontrollably and she wiped his face with her hand and said, "Don't cry." He was so amazed he stopped crying and his mother noticed him for the first time and began to talk to him.

Hannah's depth of spirit increased and she developed her own quiet passion for God. In the morning when I went downstairs to make a cup of tea, I would find her reading her Bible. In one of the worst stretches of grieving a letter arrived on the doorstep addressed to Mr. and Mrs. Williams. The familiarity of the writing disorientated us. Inside we found this:

Dear Mummy and Daddy,
I wrote this poem in spare time at school. I hope you like it.

A Journey

On a hard stormy journey,
With the wind roaring,

The clouds moving,
Sometimes you feel like giving up.
But you remember the warm end,
When you can rest.
And remember when you so nearly gave up.
But now that you have done it, it's over,
And you know that you can rest.

Love from Hannah XXXX

The poem accurately depicted our sense of journeying in grief and our longing for rest from the unrelenting fatigue of sorrow. We marveled at the depth God had planted in our daughter through her own loss.

Cerian was not only expanding our humanity; the grief of losing her was also paradoxically heightening our joy. The strange thing is, bereavement enhances our capacity for life. Not only does the fleeting nature of existence force a recognition of mortality and thus the imperative of making the most of every opportunity to love and receive love, but it also makes us cherish one another more and recognize the value of good gifts. The birth of Mark and Janet's son was just such an occasion for Paul and me.

Janet was on the seventh floor of the John Radcliffe Hospital. I had not been there since the day I visited Adrienne. I felt sick as I entered the lift. Daniel was twelve hours old. I was terrified of seeing him. I had not held a baby since Cerian. But the moment we opened the door and saw his scrunched-up little body, there was an explosion of joy. We loved him. I had to wrench Daniel away from Paul in order to hold him myself.

"Is it all right?" Janet asked.

"What do you mean, all right?" It took me a moment to register. "Oh, yes, it's all right."

Sometimes when I see Daniel, I imagine Cerian playing with him. Janet seems to know when I am thinking this and she always talks about Cerian every time our families meet. Mark and Paul had their drink together at last and again there was celebration. God gives and God takes away – it is possible for both to solicit from us the response, "Blessed be the name of the Lord" (Job 1:21).

We spent the first anniversary of Cerian's death at Wren's house. Soon after breakfast Paul and Wren disappeared to the garden center. They returned an hour or so later with a small tree cut into the shape of a bird in flight.

"The skylark!" I exclaimed when I saw them heaving it from the car into a wheelbarrow.

"Wait and see," they said. Eventually, we were allowed to look at their creation. The bird tree stood overlooking the field and below its outstretched wings Paul and Wren had gathered rocks around a tiny plaque engraved with the words:

CERIAN WILLIAMS

Loved One – Consecrated to God

We stood around the bird tree and from there I looked out over the open countryside to the sky beyond.

Some months later Wren phoned us, ecstatic. "You will never guess what has happened!"

I could not guess, but her voice sounded unusually alive. She had grieved for Cerian too, and it had taken her many months to get over the shock of nearly losing me.

"Is it a miracle?" I asked, waiting to be told.

"Yes it is. The bird tree is alive!"

I laughed.

"A pair of wrens have built a nest inside the breast of the bird tree and this morning I saw an entire family of wrens hatching. Isn't that a beautiful thing?"

It was indeed, although I couldn't trust my voice for tears, so I mumbled my agreement.

"I am going to take this as a reminder from God," said Wren. "He is able to bring life out of death, and hope out of grief."

Epilogue

I glanced at the enormous pile of books on the back seat of my car and prayed for a parking space. It was mid-June, exams were over, the undergraduates were gone, and Oxford heaved with tourists and traffic wardens. I had just finished the final draft of my book about Cerian, and I was keen to get rid of the mass of worthy tomes on prenatal screening, bioethics, and theology that had been accumulating in our dining room since her death nearly three years before. The time had come to return the books *en masse* to my college office in the center of town.

I squeezed my car into a tiny spot outside the zoology department at least half a mile from my office. Perhaps it was decadent to ask God to help me with such a small thing, but it didn't feel like an unreasonable request as I picked my way down Mansfield Road peeping over the stack of books I'd managed to wedge under my chin. I reached Holywell Street sweating profusely and barely able to resist the temptation to swear at the hordes of visitors ambling toward the city center and stopping in the middle of the pavement to photograph every historic building in sight – or at least so it seemed to me.

Two men stepped toward me. "Can we help you with those?"

"Oh my goodness, yes, thank you!" I blustered. In the apparent absence of divine help these strangers were a relief. I couldn't actually pass them the books but slowly they extracted one volume after another until the entire pile had been transferred into their arms.

"Looks like you've been busy. What's the project?" one of them asked.

"I just finished a short book on personhood, bioethics, that sort of thing." I should have known better; Oxford is not a place to be imprecise about anything, and the word "book" invited interrogation.

"Bioethics? Interesting . . . tell us more."

"Well not really bioethics as such, more a personal story addressing cultural themes."

I guided them down Broad Street, so grateful for their help that I told them the entire story from start to finish. It was only when we reached the college lodge that they told me they were bioethicists, in Oxford to attend a conference convened to discuss the effects of prenatal testing policies on women in Western and non-Western contexts.

By the time I finally slumped into my desk chair, my books safely stowed in manageable piles on the desk in front of me and my office door shut on the two strangers retreating across the quad, I realized with a degree of shock that I had agreed to address an international medical conference the following morning. I picked up the phone and confessed to Emma. I needed her help with an extra school run. I was seriously outside my comfort zone.

The first part of this book was written two years after Cerian's death, and a version was published as *The Shaming of the Strong*. Fourteen years later I have added this epilogue and revised the entire text for this second edition. I have done so because I am convinced that the central themes are even more pertinent now than when Cerian died.

We often separate stories from ideas, narratives from academic treatises, the private from the public, our hearts from our minds. I believe these dimensions always belong together; indeed, in this book broad existential questions concerning the whole of human society meet the messy realities of ordinary life.

As I look back I realize that all the work I have done as an academic since Cerian's death in 2002 has arisen out of the personal encounter described in this book. Over the last sixteen years I have often felt as if the different parts of my life were pulling in different directions – as wife, mother, daughter, citizen, historian, and teacher – but when I look back it is clear there has only ever been one journey and one question: *What does it mean to be human?* This is the question our daughter Cerian raised for me, and this is the question that lies at the core of this book.

The chance meeting with two bioethicists was my first inkling of the diverse and unexpected ways in which Cerian's story would bring me into dialogue with people I would otherwise have never met in my small Oxford bubble. Almost weekly since the original publication of Cerian's story in 2005, I have received emails and letters telling me how her short life and her death have connected with other people's experiences of grief and loss. Many parents have trusted Paul and me with stories of miscarriage and stillbirth, the deaths of children and young adults, some of

them cases of sudden death and others the long, drawn-out
agony of watching a child suffer. Many of these stories are
hard to hear, some are surprising, others shocking, most of
them contain vivid expressions of joy as well as sadness.

I think of the couple from Beijing who named their
adopted daughter Cerian, having been inspired by the
story to embrace a child with severe physical abnormalities
abandoned on the streets by her birth mother. I think
of my friend with her four-year-old daughter who has
neither speech nor physical mobility and the delight and
intimacy I see in my friend's face as she holds and cares for
her daughter. I think of another couple who, after having
been given a similar diagnosis of fetal abnormality at their
twenty-week scan, found – quite by chance – a copy of
Cerian's story in a doctor's waiting room. Having read it
they decided, come what may, to carry their son to term,
only to discover at birth that he was as healthy and robust as
could be. I think of the many couples who in spite of all the
will and desire in the world have been unable to conceive,
and those for whom Cerian's story helped them rethink
relationships with aging parents and face the realities of their
own aging process. How could I have known how deeply
Cerian's story would resonate in people's hearts?

So it is with a mixture of sadness and gratitude that I
look back on the nine months I spent with Cerian. Our
older daughters Hannah and Emilia are now leaving home.
If Cerian had lived perhaps the girls would have avoided
the layers of complex grief they both faced, and continue
to face years after Cerian's death. If Cerian had lived Paul
and I would still be going to parents' evenings at school as
well as standing in airport departure halls – lumps in our
throats and tears in our eyes – waving the girls off on their

next global adventure. Such thoughts recur intermittently to tinge each ongoing milestone with elements of grief, as they do for every family that loses a child. Nothing, however good, can ever replace a person that we love.

But it is not only the personal resonance of Cerian's story that prompts me to write about her again; it is also a deep and enduring conviction that Cerian – along with thousands like her whose physical bodies and mental capacities have never allowed them to live a so-called "normal life" – has something vital to say to a world that is restless and frantic, anxious and lonely.

The next morning Emma did the school run for me and I arrived at the medical conference in fear and trembling. For three hours I was bombarded with questions. My book-carrying friends nodded their encouragement as I struggled to answer as best I could. It was clear that my views on prenatal testing were of incidental importance to the group; their interest centered on my experience as a mother finding herself in a situation of having to decide suddenly whether or not to terminate a pregnancy. My story exemplified the stark reality that prenatal screening places some parents in the position of *having* to decide the fate of their unborn children, not merely having the *option* to do so.

"What did it feel like to be placed in this position?" All the questions came down to this one in the end. This "necessity to choose," hard though it may be for Western women used to making decisions about their own bodies, is even harder for women in parts of the Middle East, Africa, and South America. Most expectant fathers and mothers desire prenatal screening in order to check the overall health of the pregnancy for the child and the mother, but also to identify the biological sex of their child. Where in a Western context the identification of male or female is in most cases a benign advantage enabling parents to name the little person they are about to welcome into the world and to furnish a new nursery accordingly, in some non-Western contexts revealing the sex places the unborn child at risk of termination on grounds of gender, and mothers at risk of intolerable pressure to abort females.

The chief concern of everyone around the table was to understand how best to *support* women who found themselves in this invidious position. But no one asked whether this *need* to decide was a legitimate or bearable weight for parents, and especially women, to carry? No one disputed the wisdom of implementing prenatal screening programs to detect and diagnose fetal abnormalities.

As I listened to the stories of women from other parts of the world, the ordinary and routine custom of prenatal scanning that we take for granted in the West suddenly became strange to me as I saw it through fresh eyes. Built into the practice is a particular way of perceiving personhood, of defining autonomy and choice, of imagining female agency, of understanding and experiencing community, and of forming identity. The practice relies above all on a particular idea of choice and a definition of personhood in which the capacity for choice is of primary importance. Prenatal scans, though advised, are voluntary – they are customary rather than required – but it is expected nonetheless that most pregnant couples will choose to have one. The practice itself is understood to be morally neutral. It is the degree to which it supports and facilitates individual choice that determines whether or not it is good or bad, right or wrong.

As the conference went by the questions moved away from me. Being unsure exactly when I was meant to leave, I simply stayed as a fly on the wall listening to the macro-level debates into which my own tiny subjective experience fitted. I sat at the conference table feeling terribly sad as I remembered the details of Cerian's small, unlovely body. Technically speaking, during the pregnancy there were only two things we knew about her for certain – two scientifically derived facts: the fact of her physical abnormality, and the fact of her biological sex. As I listened to the debate going on around me, I wondered if it really is an advantage for these two particular facts to be the first things parents come to know about their children. What are the implications of this prior knowledge for human society?

Often couples wait to commit emotionally to their unborn child until "the viability" of a pregnancy is confirmed by means of a scan at sixteen or twenty weeks. I hear so many couples say, "We haven't told anyone yet; we're waiting until we've had the scan." They speak as if the scan determines whether or not the pregnancy is *real,* at least in a social sense; they speak as if the scan were a marker point determining whether they can lavish their love upon the child or hold it back to protect themselves. As a practice, prenatal scanning both teaches and reinforces particular ways of thinking about the human person. It teaches the pregnant couple to ask: Is this child physically normal? This question is asked as if it were of primary importance. Whether or not the scan results reveal fetal abnormality, the practice makes everyone ask this question at a relatively early stage in the pregnancy. It may only be a tiny statistical minority of parents who choose with much grief and heartache to terminate a pregnancy because of fetal abnormality (and such parents should never be judged). But the fact that we have an almost universal social practice that renders acceptable the *idea* of terminating the life of a child whose physical capacities are suboptimal affects every one of us. This idea is further reinforced by a legal structure that makes such an idea not only *plausible* but also *permissible* and *possible* right up to full term. Moreover, we have sophisticated language to cloak the idea in moral neutrality, and we have a definition of "quality of life" to explain why such an idea is right and necessary.

But do we ever ask whether this idea is *just*? Is it *just* for the majority of people to condone a social practice that permits a few to be treated in ways the majority would never permit for themselves? Would the majority of people want to be asked, before they were treated with equal dignity and respect, if they have a normal body, or if they are female? To condone this treatment for some not only dehumanizes those who are never born, it dehumanizes all of us. To make human personhood contingent in any way upon physical "normality" is to strip all of us of our inherent and intrinsic worth as persons.

In the same way we never ask whether the practice of prenatal screening is actually *good* for a society. The social practices in which we participate establish the ground rules for us all. They establish an evaluative grid of "normality" through which we filter our self-understanding, our value, and our sense of worth. With such a grid it is no wonder that every piece of evidence suggests that as a society we are becoming more anxious, restless, and lonely than ever before. Such an evaluative grid makes it harder, not easier, for us to care for one another, especially the physically impaired, the mentally ill, and the vulnerable. It makes it harder, not easier, for those who are aging to accept the inevitable limitation that aging brings, and for the rest of us to honor our loved ones when their physical capacities diminish. It makes it harder, not easier, for us to live interdependent, mutually sustaining lives in family units, in local communities, and in civil societies.

Over the years I have reflected deeply on the weeks and months I spent with Cerian. That period of time felt like an age when I was in the midst of it, but in the scheme of things it was so short. I cannot help but think how easily I might have missed the beauty and the privilege of that time with her. This time of limitation and vulnerability was also a time of profound humanity during which I discovered my need of God, but also my need of others, and their need of me. For nine months only, every human being has the one chance they will ever have of being received first and foremost as a person before *anything else* is known about them. At a time when so many young people struggle intensely with their physicality, with their male or female bodies, with their identities as sexual beings, with the health and appearance of their body, the nine months of pregnancy may be the only opportunity we will have as parents to receive our child simply as a person of equal, inviolable worth whether they turn out to be healthy or sick, male or female, attractive or plain. Why are we choosing to rob ourselves of this extraordinary and unique gift?

I left that conference acutely conscious of my responsibility as a member of society. Listening to the debates relocated Cerian's story in a much larger social drama. It showed me that my personal and at times self-referential perspective, my private autonomous decisions to act in certain ways, have real consequences for society as a whole

whether I recognize it or not. Seismic changes in the history
of human civilization happen one day at a time, with tiny
movements of individual human hearts and with small,
seemingly insignificant changes in language and actions.

During the years since Cerian's death, notions of individual
agency and choice have become even more deeply inter-
twined with cultural definitions of personhood, sex, gender,
conception, pregnancy, and birth; with the ways in which
we perceive our bodies and appreciate beauty; and with
aging, physical decay, and dying itself. We are saturated with
the assumption that we can and will choose the timing of
birth, the number of children we have, and increasingly the
gender and the genetic makeup of the child that we desire.
We make choices as individuals to have sex with partners of
our choosing and we choose whether or not this act will lead
to conception. Precious though we all understand children
to be, we behave as if they were commodities – commodities
that we acquire as an extension of ourselves. We have grown
familiar with the idea of conferring personhood selectively
on the ones we choose at the time we choose them in the
form we find desirable, preferable, and acceptable. Indeed,
in the Western world, *choosing what we desire* has become the
essence of what it means to be human.

   We are faced with mounting pressure to establish the
social practice of assisted dying. As in the case of termination
for fetal abnormality, it may only be a tiny number of
people who choose to determine the manner and timing
of their death, but as a social practice the *idea* of assisted
dying nonetheless makes it possible for every person to ask
themselves: Do I want to live when I am no longer useful to
society and helpful to my family? Do I have value, worth,

and dignity as a person if I cease to be independent and able
to make choices for myself? We already have the language to
legitimate the practice of assisted dying as morally neutral.
We have a socially acceptable definition of "quality of life"
to explain why such a practice might be good and even
necessary and why scarce resources should be diverted from
the incapacitated to maximize opportunities for younger
members of society. We live in societies overwhelmed by
the challenges of social care. These challenges are economic
but they also represent a crisis of responsibility. In a culture
that prizes autonomous individual choice over communal
relationships, whose responsibility is it to care for the elderly,
the vulnerable, the homeless, and the sick? In such a climate
it would take very little to develop a social expectation that it
is *right* and *moral* to provide everyone with the option to die
with dignity – with dignity defined as the ability to control
and determine the end of one's life.

Our society tells us that our choices are unlimited, that
choice is the means to human flourishing, that to have
one's choices impaired is to be dehumanized. As a society
we try to deal with suffering by controlling it, mastering it,
and seeking to eliminate it. If we fail in this endeavor, then
at least we hide it, we silence the mention of it, we insure
heavily against it, we insulate ourselves from it, we resolve
to ignore it. We mask the reality of death.

And yet this idea of humanness defined by choice, into
which we are all baptized, does not line up with our messy,
complicated, everyday humanness. It has nothing to say
when aging creeps into our bones, wrinkles our skin, reduces
our eyesight, and limits our energy. It has no dignity to give
us when we become dependent on others, and no dignity
to give to those who care for others. It has no time beyond

the moment, and no validity beyond experience. It does not prepare us for the powerlessness that comes to all of us when our choices fail, when the scope of choice narrows, when our choices are overlooked, violated, or curtailed by others.

For all our elevation of choice we find it harder to live with the choices we have made, and with the bodies we do have – whether male or female. We find it harder to handle our finitude, our limitation, and our weakness, and we have little to offer one another in the face of pain. We trade enduring community for an association of eclectic "friends" with whom we align ourselves because we meet the entry requirements, and from whose company we know deep down we will be ejected when we are no longer acceptable.

We are promised autonomy but find ourselves lonely. We are promised uniqueness but are given an identity brand. What we think of as freedom of choice rapidly becomes dependency on consumption for meaning and identity as human beings. We go into debt to provide our children with the things we think they must have and drive them to maximize their potential through education and grade performance to perpetuate the lifestyle dreams that we have for them. We know this is a dangerous road but it is so wide and familiar and "normal" that we run down it fearlessly without a second thought as to where it might lead us in the end.

It is a tragic irony that we who believe so vehemently in choice rarely use the choices we do have to bring about lasting change. We believe in human agency and yet we don't believe we can make a difference. We cower before a system that seems impossible to change, resign ourselves to silence, or simply become too busy and preoccupied. We are trapped in the contradictions of the world we have created for ourselves.

Against this backdrop, the quiet beauty of Cerian's life goes on challenging me: *What does it really mean to be human?* Cerian didn't have any choices, and yet she was perfectly human.

The overriding memory of my time with Cerian, the one I will carry with me for the rest of my life, was the glimpse I had, during the moments of her death, of the love and glory of God. That memory causes all the other recollections, good and bad, to pale in comparison. God the creator came in his love to take a vulnerable human being home to be with him. This encounter changed my life. Quite simply, it showed me that there is another way to be in the world.

Limitation, finitude, suffering, weakness, disability, and frailty can be gifts. Far from robbing us of our humanity, without a place for these things we are less than human. Ultimately, personhood is not a work of self-definition and self-creation. Instead, it is a gift.

The Creator who gave us this gift did not leave us to the mercy of ourselves. He does not leave us trapped in the contradictions of the world we create. Instead, he freely chose to limit himself, taking on – as it says in Philippians 2 – the very nature of a servant. He identified himself with the weak, the sick, the poor, and the vulnerable – even more so, he *became* all these things for us. On the cross he took the full force of termination into his own body. He was disposed of by his culture. He did not avoid suffering, he embraced it. And in facing suffering and limitation he changed the meaning of it for all of us. He makes the promise of freedom without limitation hollow, love without cost meaningless.

He calls weakness strength; death he calls life; the things we discard he calls valuable.

As a result of this extraordinary love we are able in our human limitation to point beyond ourselves to a God who is with us, and will never leave us. We are given the strength to set aside our own preferences and preoccupations for the sake of others. Our need of one another can teach us what it means to belong. Our suffering can enable us to recognize joy. Loss and grief, imperfection and brokenness can help us accept that we are each perfectly human – nothing more and nothing less.

Related Titles

Be Not Afraid: Overcoming the Fear of Death
Johann Christoph Arnold

You Carried Me: A Daughter's Memoir
Melissa Ohden

Why Children Matter
Johann Christoph Arnold

Their Name Is Today: Reclaiming Childhood in a Hostile World
Johann Christoph Arnold

Rich in Years: Finding Peace and Purpose in a Long Life
Johann Christoph Arnold

PLOUGH PUBLISHING HOUSE
151 Bowne Drive, PO BOX 398, Walden, NY 12586, USA
Brightling Road, Robertsbridge, East Sussex TN32 5DR, UK
4188 Gwydir Highway, Elsmore, NSW 2360, Australia
845-572-3455 • info@plough.com • www.plough.com